Ashes t

Martin Dudley was born in Birmingham and educated at King Edward's School. He studied theology at King's College, London, and has a doctorate in theology. Ordained in Wales, he has been a parish priest for twenty years and is now Rector of St Bartholomew the Great, Smithfield, in the City of London. A Fellow of the Society of Antiquaries and of the Royal Historical Society, he has edited and contributed to a number of books on theology, history and liturgy including, most recently, *A Manual for Ministry to the Sick* (SPCK) and *Humanity and Healing* (DLT).

Ashes to Glory

MEDITATIONS FOR LENT, HOLY WEEK AND EASTER

Martin Dudley

First published in Great Britain in 1999 by
SPCK
Holy Trinity Church, Marylebone Road,
London NW1 4DU

© Martin Dudley 1999

All rights reserved. No part of this book may be reproduced
or transmitted in any form or by any means, electronic or
mechanical, including photocopying, recording, or by any
information storage and retrieval system, without
permission in writing from the publisher.

Unless otherwise stated, quotations from Scripture are taken
from *The New Revised Standard Version of the Bible* © 1989.
The Revised Standard Version of the Bible is copyright © 1971
and 1952. Quotations from the Psalms are taken from the
Book of Common Prayer of 1662, the rights of which are vested
in the Crown in perpetuity within the United Kingdom.

British Library Cataloguing-in-Publication Data

A catalogue record for this book is available from
the British Library

ISBN 0-281-05247-6

Typeset by Pioneer Associates, Perthshire
Printed in Great Britain by
Caledonian International, Bishopbriggs, Glasgow

Dedicated with grateful thanks to my
congregations at

St Mary's, Whitchurch, Cardiff

Holy Trinity, Weston

St Lawrence, Ardeley

St George in Owlsmoor

St Bartholomew the Great, Smithfield

CONTENTS

PREFACE

'I invite you, therefore, in the name of the Church, to the observance of a holy Lent.' These words will probably be addressed to you during the Ash Wednesday liturgy at the very beginning of the Church's preparation for Easter. And I invite you to keep Lent with me by using the meditations and reflections gathered in this little book and by joining me in an act of spiritual pilgrimage that takes us from the ashes placed on our heads as a sign of our mortality to the glory we have as we rise with Christ.

In each of my twenty years of ordained ministry I have preached through Lent, Holy Week and Easter and also met with small groups to explore aspects of our faith and worship. This book emerges from that experience in which so many have shared, and the value that I hope it has for the reader is very much the result of conversations with parishioners about the meaning of Lent and the profound significance of Christ's Passion, death and resurrection.

This book can be used for individual prayer and thought; it can also be used by groups. There are some suggested topics for discussion included at the end of the book. Unlike most Lent courses, it goes right through to Easter, and if it is used by a group I think it important to carry on through and to meet again after experiencing the Holy Week and Easter liturgy.

One prayer informs much of my thinking and I ask you to use it as you pray this Lent. It was written by the American priest and liturgist William Reed Huntington and included in his *Materia Ritualis* of 1882. It was proposed for inclusion in the 1892 revision of the *American Prayer Book*, but was not included until the revision of 1928 as the collect for the Monday of Holy Week. It was retained in the 1979 book and became the collect for Lent 3 in the Alternative Service Book (ASB) and has kept its place in the most recent revision.

Almighty God, whose most dear Son went not up to joy but first he suffered pain and entered not into glory before he was crucified; Mercifully grant that we, walking in the way of the cross may find it none other than the way of life and peace; through the same thy Son Jesus Christ our Lord.

I pray that you may share this experience and following in his footsteps may find life and peace in him.

Martin Dudley
The Feast of the Epiphany 1999

PROLOGUE:
Penitence requires preparation

Near to the end of Lent, as it reaches its climax and dramatic conclusion, you will probably find yourself singing a hymn by Theodulph, Bishop of Orléans. 'All glory, laud, and honour to thee, Redeemer King' is John Mason Neale's translation of the Palm Sunday hymn which he probably wrote while in exile from Charlemagne's court in the early ninth century. That hymn, sung as we carry our palms in procession, expresses by both words and music the nature of our celebration of the Passion. Theodulph was Abbot of Fleury-sur-Loire (now called St Benoit, for St Benedict's bones rest there) and then joined Alcuin of York at Aachen, until he was made a bishop in 798. Charlemagne was committed to the reform of the Church and was intent on using it as the means to bind his empire together. Within a very few years of becoming a bishop, Theodulph issued a set of precepts to the priests of his diocese urging them to holiness of living and to dedicated service. It set out a number of matters that they were to teach to their people. Some of these precepts concern the observance of Lent.

Theodulph's first instruction is that, one week before the beginning of Lent, the faithful should make their confessions to the priests, penance should be received, quarrels resolved, all disputes settled, and from their hearts the people were to forgive the offences of others so that they might freely say, 'Forgive us our trespasses as we forgive them that trespass against us.' With great pastoral wisdom, Theodulph shows that penitence is not just about being right with God and cannot just be limited to a liturgy or sacramental rite in church. It involves apologies, recompense, reconciliation, forgiving others and allowing ourselves to be forgiven. Then we may enter upon the blessed Lenten season and may, with clear and purified hearts, approach the most holy feast of Easter.

Theodulph's precepts form a prologue to this little book of Lenten meditations because it is not enough for us to start off on Ash Wednesday. Penitence requires preparation. Shrove Tuesday completed the process of being shriven, of confessing and receiving forgiveness so that Lent itself might be a holy time. Lent requires some rules, some consideration well in advance of how it is going to be kept. Churches frequently offer Lent courses. Often these are educational. They may be good and useful, but Lent is not primarily about education.

Lent, Theodulph explains, is a fast – a time in which we limit our intake of food, taking only one meal a day. He takes this very seriously. These days of Lent are, he says, the tithes of our year, the tenth offered to God; forty days out of nearly four hundred which we should pass with all devotion and sanctity. He stresses that this is not a fast undertaken by the will of the individual but one determined and hallowed by God. He then sets out the ways in which Lent should be kept:

- it should include charity, giving alms to the poor.
- it should not involve missing lunch and eating a double portion for dinner.
- it should include prayer.
- it should involve abstention from pleasure.
- it should be a time of chaste and sober living.
- it should include abstention from eggs, meat, cheese, fish and wine, but fasting and abstention should be sensible and Theodulph recommends a little wine at the end of the day to restore the body so long as it does not lead to drunkenness.

- the sacrament of Christ's body and blood should be received every Sunday.
- there should be no quarrels or lawsuits but all should continue in the praise of God and in the doing of necessary work.

This then is Theodulph's vision of Lent. We need to have our own vision of Lent. Whatever it is, it should make a difference to our daily living. We may stress rather different things from those that seemed essential in the early ninth century and Theodulph need not be our model – though he speaks a lot of sense. What is important is that we do *something* that counts, and it is surely better to draw on the great tradition to which we belong rather than to invent something new and untried.

Our Lenten meditations begin with our mortality, with the recognition of the unequal relationship between the creature and the Creator, before we come to consider what discipleship means and how we are able to follow Jesus on the journey that leads to death and resurrection. There is a meditation for every day and extra ones for Holy Week and Easter. There are many themes running through Lent and I have not tied myself rigidly to any one of them. The pilgrim, following in the Master's footsteps, will muse of many things and see many sights. There will be times of joy when we seem fully to grasp what we are about – and be grasped by it – and there are times when it all seems pointless. There will be times when we need to listen to stories, and perhaps tell our own; times when we feel able to wrestle with complex ideas, and times when we need silence. All these aspects will be found here. I hope that my reflections – emerging from daily living, from reading, and prayer, and from the liturgy – will provide a companion for your journey.

ASH WEDNESDAY:
Humble yourselves before the Lord

'For everyone who exalts himself will be humbled, and he who humbles himself will be exalted' (Luke 14.11, RSV). These words of Jesus should be set alongside those found in the Letter of James: 'Humble yourselves before the Lord, and he will exalt you' (James 4.10). They need this gloss, this expansion and commentary, because Jesus' own words are familiar to us but we often fail to grasp what they mean or to act upon them. If these words could be likened to the seed that the sower casts, then we would have to concede that they have fallen on stony ground or else that the cares and pleasures of this world, like weeds and thistles, have overwhelmed them. The key words of our Western culture at the end of the century are 'luxurious', 'prestigious' and 'exclusive'. This is not likely to create an environment in which humbleness is valued. If you have what the world wants, flaunt it, exalt in it, make your neighbours envious of it!

We know that such behaviour is often a pretence, a false bolstering up, claiming more for oneself in the hope that that is how it will be. To him who has – or seems to have – shall more be given. Against this we hear the oft-repeated refrain of the funeral service: earth to earth, ashes to ashes, dust to dust. Houses decay, cars rust, memories tarnish, and we too are perishable, dust returning to dust. We do not exist of ourselves. We cannot by effort, thought, or will-power make ourselves taller, count the number of hairs on our heads, or extend our lives. All that we are comes from outside us, and yet we are full of pretensions, pride and vanities of every sort. We have not learned the lesson of Job, whom God addressed in these words:

Who is this that darkens counsel by words without
   knowledge? . . .
I will question you, and you shall declare to me.
Where were you when I laid the foundation of
   the earth?
Tell me, if you have understanding.
Who determined its measurements – surely you know!
Or who stretched the line upon it?
On what were its bases sunk, or who laid its
   cornerstone,
when the morning stars sang together,
and all the sons of God shouted for joy?

(Job 38.2–7, RSV)

Job at least acknowledged that he was of small account, that
he had uttered what he did not understand, and made light of
God. Job at least, when the truth was revealed to him of the
distance between him and the Holy One whom angels worship, despised himself and repented in dust and ashes. We have
to be persuaded of the need for such humility. Like the Pharisee
in the parable of the Pharisee and the tax collector (Luke
18.9–14) we count up what we do, what makes us different,
our kindness, our generosity, our good works. Lent is intended
to pull us up, to stop us in our tracks, and to enable us to check,
to evaluate our attitude to God. If we do not take notice, we
are like the person who sees a warning about high voltage
and danger of death and thinks that it is a clock battery.

    We cannot plead ignorance. We cannot say, 'I did not
know.' For we *do* know that the God whom we worship is
the All-Holy, the Creator, the Ancient of Days, awful in
majesty, the one to whom all hearts are open and all desires
known, who made the heavens and the earth, and created all
that is, visible and invisible. Before him is a devouring fire,

round about him a mighty tempest. And it is this Lord who asks what right we have to recite his statutes or to take his covenant on our lips.

> For you hate discipline,
>> and you cast my words behind you.
> You make friends with a thief when you see one,
>> and you keep company with adulterers.
> You give your mouth free rein for evil,
>> and your tongue frames deceit . . .
> These things you have done and I have been silent;
>> you thought that I was one just like yourself.
> But now I rebuke you, and lay the charge before you.
>> (Psalm 50.17–21)

Why does the tax gatherer go home acquitted? Because of his realism and his honesty. He keeps his distance. He does not raise his eyes to heaven. He beats his breast. He humbles himself, and the Lord Almighty does not despise a contrite heart. But he abhors self-righteousness and hypocrisy, the hypocrisy that expresses belief and trust in God, that confesses him as Lord, and yet no aspect of life is thereby changed. Should we not do for God at least some portion of what we readily do for ourselves and for others when the fancy takes us? For pleasure, for shopping, to visit friends, to satisfy some whim, we will give up time and expend energy, in comparison with which what we offer God is insulting, derisory, contemptible.

Remember that you are dust, and to dust you will return. When we grasp that, when we confront our mortality, when we know what we really are, we will cease from exaltation, turn humbly to God and put our trust in him.

THURSDAY AFTER ASH WEDNESDAY:
It is worth trusting in God

If I had just a very few minutes to make a definitive testimony I would say this — *it is worth trusting in God*. I would say that first of all because I believe it without reservation. I must confess that there are a lot of other things that I believe with a reservation or two. And second, I would say it because, in my experience, it is true. Quite apart from my own experience of being called by God, shaken by God, and restored by God — an experience whose subjectivity I frankly acknowledge — my basic premise, that it is worth trusting in God, can be unpacked in a coherent and reasonable way.

The one I recommend you to trust in — the one we call God, the Deity, the Divine Majesty, the Creator, *Theos, Deus, Gott, Dieu, Duw* — is the one Jesus called Father and who called Jesus his Son, the Beloved. This is not some remote, disinterested deity — this is God the Creator bound up with the creation. This is the God of the covenant with Noah, with Abraham, with Jacob, with Moses. And this bond, this commitment, reaches its conclusion, its highest and definitive point, in the incarnation, when God takes our nature and becomes man, for us and for our salvation. For this reason Jesus also is called God — God from God, Light from Light, Very God of Very God. Yet there is one God and it is this one God in whom you should trust.

This is not a relation of equals. There is no equality between the Creator and the creature, the immortal and the mortal, the eternal and the transient, the necessary and the contingent. Quite the contrary. God is love, and we so rarely love and are so often filled with hatred. God is just, and we are unjust. God is light, and we love darkness. God is life, and our lot has become death, separated by sin, by wilful disobedience and rejection, from the source of life. But all is not lost, for Christ, God for us, suffered for our sins, once and for all, in order that we might be brought back to God, in order that we might be reconciled to him.

It is worth trusting in God because only when we trust him can we make sense of our odd, pointless, disordered lives. When we trust, making a step of faith, letting go of certainties and accepting promises, we pass definitively into a different order of existence. It is marked by its orientation towards God.

It is worth trusting God for the present and not only for the future. Only in God can we understand who we are and what it means to be human. Only God remains unchanged by our failings, our infidelities, our foolishness. Only God loves us unreservedly and unconditionally, making loveable that which seems unlovely. Only God can do this and that is why my message would be: it is worth trusting in God.

FRIDAY AFTER ASH WEDNESDAY:
We are among those who have faith

Faith is not about content but about attitude. There is a content to the Christian faith. We can write it down. It is available for comment and discussion. We can say, 'This is the faith of the Church' but the real statement of faith begins, 'I believe.' Faith is not something done to me or for me, but something I do — I believe. For the great majority of people, faith doesn't happen spontaneously, any more than we wake up one day and find that without teaching or preparation we can read or write. We grow into faith. We won't find faith in God if we have not learned that faith in human beings is not ill-founded. Learning to trust is a preamble to faith. When Jesus elicited faith, it was because of who he was and how he spoke rather than what he spoke. He spoke with authority, with such evident transparent sincerity and conviction that, from those who had not prejudged him, he drew forth the response of faith. Faith is belief made real through trust; it is belief in action.

The Letter to the Hebrews speaks of confidence and of the trust in God that facilitates action (Hebrews 3.6, 14; 10.35). Loss of confidence strips us of power. It can even make the daily round of living impossible. The confidence that is based on faith and trust in God makes all things possible within the will of God. We are to live by this faith. That is to say, as those who have faith, we are not merely to confess it but to shape our lives by it. So what is it that guides us? It is belief and trust in God, the Divine Origin of all that is, the profoundly Other who is present to us, the ground and foundation of our being, the ultimate source of all things, the one in whom we live and move and have our being.

I can believe in God in the same way I believe in the outer planets of our solar system – Jupiter, 483.6 million miles from the sun, circling it every twelve years or thereabouts, or, further out, Pluto, 3,675 million miles from the sun, spending 248.5 years in its orbit. I believe what the encyclopaedia tells me about them and I am amazed by the distances and time periods involved but my life is not in any way different because of my belief. I can treat belief in God in much the same way, but as I come to trust God, to contemplate what it means that God's nature is revealed to us in Christ; when I ponder the meaning of incarnation, the enfleshing of God, for us and for our salvation; then I find the credal formula, the 'I believe', becomes a part of the essential structure of my life. When that happens, I can act out of faith and not shrink from the challenges of faith.

SATURDAY AFTER ASH WEDNESDAY:
Faith needs discipline

A novel of Japanese martial arts would not normally have been on my reading list. It surprises me even now that I read it. I had enjoyed Jay McInerney's later work and found his early novels remaindered in a shop near Waterloo Station. Unable to resist a bargain, I bought three of them. I started this one with some reservations but found it totally engrossing. It was the story of a young American who flees to Japan and seeks admission to a martial arts group. He is initially rejected by the *sensei*, the master and teacher, and by the *dojo*, the group of disciples. This young American, Ransom by name, had, until this point, drifted across continents and oceans, across varying diverse landscapes, oblivious to almost everything except his own pain and guilt. He had watched the practice sessions of the *dojo* for a week and found it, with its strange incantations and white uniforms, a sacramental place, an intersection of body and spirit, where power and danger and will were ritualized in such a way that a man could learn to understand them. Ransom, we are told, had lost his bearings spiritually, and he wanted to reclaim himself.

It wasn't easy. The *sensei* didn't want him. Undeterred, Ransom kept coming back. After three nights he was accepted for training but it would be a long time before he could begin the karate. First he had to learn the technique of sweeping the practice yard and the art of bowing. It seemed easy. It wasn't. He was convinced that he was being systematically humiliated. He wasn't. He had begun the process of learning, the process we call discipleship.

Today we place a great stress on individual freedom, on choice and opportunity. The annual catalogues of courses offered by countless institutions provide us with the opportunity to learn about almost everything. The spiritually disoriented can choose from an extraordinary variety of religious traditions – a variety so great that it actually increases the sense of being disoriented. The questions become pressing: which tradition, church, cult, sect, denomination or religion expresses the fullness of truth? Clearly one does not find out by a taster, by a short course. The inner nature of a religious tradition is unfolded to and for the disciple. Being a disciple means staying with it, hanging on through periods of aridity, perplexity and confusion, to a teacher and a teaching. Being a disciple certainly involves choice but the choosing is not mine alone – I must also be chosen.

The way of the disciple involves discipline. There is a stage, more or less prolonged, in which that discipline no matter how inconvenient must be accepted, for it leads to a greater freedom. Within the intertwined Anglican and Catholic traditions of Christianity we have to learn about the nature of worship, of corporate rather than private prayer. We have also to learn about the corporate nature of faith, the 'we believe' and the 'we confess' in relation to 'I believe' and 'I confess'. And in places of traditional, formal worship we may need to learn how buildings and rites and ceremonies mediate the divine presence and how music leads us closer to God. We have to understand how the tradition enables and does not inhibit the present and the future. And this is necessary because here is a path – one path among many – of discipleship.

Perhaps those who want to follow the Christian path of discipleship should be kept outside for a time – there is good precedent for this in the early Church – to ensure that they truly desire to enter. Perhaps we should even insist that they learn how to sweep the floor of the worship space and learn by constant repetition the arts of bowing, genuflecting and kneeling, of bowing the head at the name of Jesus, and making the sign of the cross. Perhaps we do not ask enough of those who would be Christ's disciples and do not ourselves accept willingly the discipline of the way. Yet there is also a tradition of openness, of allowing people to share in worship, in the hope and expectation that there they will catch a glimpse of divine glory and accept the call to discipleship. It is harder to be open than to be closed because openness acknowledges that it is not our task to call or to choose. That belongs to the only true Master, who has called and chosen us.

FIRST SUNDAY OF LENT:
By faith Noah took heed and constructed an ark

My younger son is fascinated by the simple, cardboard Noah's ark that his mother has made for him. He loves to move the people and the animals around and to show how the food is loaded on board. He is unaware, as so many are today, of the full story of Noah and the flood as set out in Genesis. It is a long story, taking up four chapters, but we cannot understand its significance for the story of salvation or for the liturgy unless we have read it. It begins in Genesis 6.

The first section consists of a very ancient piece of folklore giving an account of life between the fall and the flood and suggestive of a diversity of higher life forms. There are at least three basic types of being mentioned here: men and with them the fair daughters of men; the sons of God; and the Nephilim, who were the product of the joining of the sons of God with the daughters of men, the mighty men of old, the men of renown. The Hebrew *nephilim* is rendered into Greek, Latin and English as 'the giants'. We may feel as we hear this story that we are drifting off into alien cosmologies, into accounts of creation that involve the cosmic interplay between different gods – gods of earth and sky and water and more – a whole series of youthful, turbulent deities, such as we find in Mesopotamian accounts of creation and flood, like the Epic of Gilgamesh. Ultimately these stories, old as they are, are of no account for our purposes – they do not contribute to the history of salvation. We may be fascinated and tantalized by a passing reference to a race of giants, and the reference is the more significant because there are so few of these strongly mythical references in the extant text of Genesis, but what it says is that God decided to bring this first attempt at populating the world to an end and so cuts off the lines of giants.

It is human depravity that gives God reason to bring about the flood. A Babylonian epic sees the flood as the gods' answer to human noise. I don't think there is much point denying a strong relationship between the Babylonian sources and Genesis. Enki or Ea – lord of the earth and of the under-world, god of water and wisdom – reveals to Ut-napishtim – the Babylonian Noah – the intention of Enlil the storm god to drown mankind in a great flood. Ea gives instructions for the building of a boat in which Ut-napishtim and his family are saved. These various accounts bear testimony to the experience of a great flood in all the known world some-where about 3000 BC. Archaeology reveals a significant layer of water-worn sand at a number of Mesopotamian sites, separating levels of remains of civilization. It is likely that there were a number of floods, and that the memory of them was etched into the religious consciousness of those peoples and preserved in their writings.

What is profoundly different about Genesis is the absence of conflict between different gods, and the way in which the Lord God takes full responsibility for this action and himself chooses Noah and his family to provide the new beginning. This account is woven into the Hebrew understanding of covenant and the Christian understanding of the relation between creature and Creator. As Hebrews says: 'By faith Noah, warned by God about events as yet unseen, respected the warning and built an ark to save his household; by this he condemned the world and became an heir to the righteousness that is in accordance with faith' (Hebrews 11.7).

There is the reference to Noah in 1 Peter 3.20–1 in which we are told how Jesus went and preached to the spirits in prison 'who in former times did not obey, when God waited patiently in the days of Noah, during the building of the ark, in which a few, that is, eight people, were saved through water. And baptism, which this prefigured, now saves you.' These imprisoned spirits have been read as the 'sons of God' who took human wives, fallen angels or demons, and who would not, in the end, listen to Christ either. This interpretation is reinforced by 2 Peter 2 in which the angels who sinned are cast into pits of nether gloom but Noah, a herald of righteousness, is preserved with seven other persons. Baptism is interpreted as the new flood, destroying the old man and the former sin-laden humanity, and bringing about a new creation. Thus it parallels the destruction of all humankind except for those in the ark and the initiation of a new world – not a new creation *ex nihilo*, like the first creation, but one that continues by redemption what has already come into being. Noah, therefore, prefigures Christ, as the ark itself prefigures the Church, the vessel of salvation.

MONDAY OF THE FIRST WEEK:
After the flood

On holiday in France among the vineyards of Touraine, the area south of the Loire near Tours where it is said that St Martin was the first to learn the value of pruning vines, I was delighted by the great carved head, crowned with grapes, that surmounted the door to Cardinal de Richelieu's wine cellar, all that remains of his chateau. It was Bacchus, but it could have been Noah for Scripture is adamant that Noah was the first tiller of the soil after the flood, that Noah planted a vineyard and that Noah got drunk. As I thought on that I recalled an index entry in the Zohar concerning Noah after the flood. The Zohar is a major text of that Jewish mystical tradition called the Kabbalah. Gershom Scholem, the outstanding authority on Jewish mysticism, called it 'the most famous and influential book of [Jewish] mystical literature'. It claims to be an ancient work of the Rabbi Shim'on of Yohai but it made its first appearance in thirteenth-century Spain, where Christian, Arabic and Jewish traditions intermingled. I know little of its complex theosophical ideas but I was struck by what it had to say about Noah – particularly struck because of the way in which Christianity, as we have seen, treats Noah as a type of Christ and the saving ark as a type of the Church.

In the section of the Zohar headed 'After the flood', the rabbi glosses the text; that is to say, using the rabbinic tradition of elaborated commentary, he expands on the events. Noah comes out from the ark, sees the world completely destroyed and begins crying for the world. He berates God, sounding rather like Job: 'Master of the world! If you destroyed your world because of human sin or human fools, then why did you create them? One or the other you should do: either do not create the human being or do not destroy the world!' Then Noah offered his sacrifice and began to pray, and 'the aroma ascended before the Blessed Holy One and was sweet'. But this is not an end of it, for the rabbis wished to know, as we might, how God responded to Noah when he saw the whole world destroyed and began to cry over the holocaust. They held that God rebuked Noah:

> The Blessed Holy One answered him: 'Foolish shepherd! Now you say this, but not when I spoke to you tenderly, saying "Make an ark of gopher wood . . ." When I said, As for me, I am about to bring the Flood . . . to destroy all flesh. When I said that you were to go into the ark, because I had found you alone to be righteous. I lingered with you and spoke at length, so that you would ask for mercy for the world! But as soon as you heard that you would be safe in the ark, the evil world did not touch your heart. You built the ark and saved yourself. Now that the world has been destroyed you open your mouth to utter questions and pleas.'

So Rabbi Yohanan taught that there was a great difference between Noah and the righteous heroes of Israel. Noah did not shield his generation and did not pray for them like Abraham at the oaks of Mamre when God revealed his intention to destroy Sodom and Gomorrah. He did not argue with God. He did not care to seek mercy for his generation; he just built the ark and the whole world was destroyed.

There is a great difference – a very great difference – between the words of the Epistle to the Hebrews and of the

Zohar. The writer to the Hebrews holds Noah up as an example of faith: 'By faith Noah, warned by God about events as yet unseen, respected the warning and built an ark to save his household; by this he condemned the world and became an heir to the righteousness that is in accordance with faith' (Hebrews 11.7).

Zohar and Hebrews agree that Noah condemned the world. The New Testament sees this as a good thing. The rabbis see it as a weakness, a failure, as selfishness. The New Testament puts Noah near the beginning of the great procession of those who have acted in faith, following the promises of God. The Zohar excludes him from the heroes precisely because he is seen as acting for himself and not for the world. The hero of the persecuting Christians cannot be the hero of the persecuted Jews.

The waters that brought death to the world were the same waters that upheld the saving home of Noah and his family. The God who destroys is the God who saves. This is a difficulty that we cannot evade or avoid. Life and death are both in God's hands and though we may be like God, God is not like us. The divine will is beyond human logic, beyond human comprehension.

TUESDAY OF THE FIRST WEEK:
You are my Son, the Beloved

Sunday's gospel — Mark's account of the baptism of Jesus — has already been heard this year on the Sunday after the Epiphany, observed as the feast of the baptism of the Lord. There it was seen as part of the process by which the divine nature of the child born to Mary in Bethlehem was made known. As Bishop Christopher Wordsworth's familiar hymn reminds us, Jesus was 'manifest at Jordan's stream, Prophet, Priest, and King supreme . . . God in Man made manifest'. The unity of the liturgical cycle is well demonstrated here. The feast of Christ's baptism looked back to the repentance preached by John the Baptist, one of the Advent themes. The first Sunday of Lent looks onwards to the temptation in the wilderness — the forty days which, in part, inspire our own Lenten observance — and to the Lord's conflict with the father of lies.

The pivotal point is the moment after his baptism by John in the Jordan when, as Jesus rises from the water, he is anointed with the Holy Spirit and affirmed as the Beloved Son. This is the point at which Jesus' ministry begins. We are, remember, only ten verses into the Gospel according to St Mark. Baptism, for us, is the occasion when Christ claims us as his own, and calls us his beloved ones. If we were baptized as babies or children, it may be some years before the sacramental grace that flooded us at that time shows its true effect. When we affirm in the liturgy (on Easter Day perhaps) the baptismal covenant made on our behalf, or make it ourselves in adult baptism, we recognize the call to ministry, the identification with Christ.

The renewal of the baptismal covenant, like baptism itself, involves renunciation of all that is opposed to God. This is expressed as renunciation of the devil or Satan, as well as of the snares and delusions of the world and the flesh.

Jesus always acted freely. He was not compelled to do the will of his Father but freely chose to do so. The Spirit, preparing him for the final conflict, drives him into the desert to face the tests involved in being alone, in being in the wilderness, in fasting, and in being tempted by Satan. In other words, Jesus' experience expresses the reality of our renunciations. As we affirm our discipleship we must expect to face the temptations, the tests of the sincerity of our commitment. The untried soldier presents a risk in battle; so does the untried Christian in a frequently inhospitable world. If we are not to retreat into some sort of ghetto mentality, in which the world is divided into those who are Christians, really born-again Christians who can be our friends, and non-Christians (including those who subscribe to a different sort of Christianity from our own) who must be converted, then we must accept the testing of our discipleship and show ourselves faithful in small things before we aspire to the greater.

WEDNESDAY OF THE FIRST WEEK:
You are a new creation

Right at the beginning of his first letter to the Christians in Corinth, the Apostle Paul reminds them of the need for unity of mind and purpose in the church, for he has heard from Chloe's people that there are quarrels among his brothers and sisters in the faith (1 Corinthians 1.10–17). If we date this letter at about AD 52 and reckon that Paul founded the church there in AD 50, then we can see how easily and how quickly divisions can arise. You probably remember the initial problem. Some are saying, 'I belong to Paul', others 'I belong to Apollos', or again 'I belong to Cephas' (that is, Peter), and some, more wisely, are saying, 'I belong to Christ'. Paul asks, 'Has Christ been divided? Was Paul crucified for you? Were you baptized in the name of Paul?' And he goes on to say that he is glad that he baptized no one, except for Crispus and Gaius, and then he remembers that he also baptized the household of Stephanas, and he eventually admits that he can't remember whether he baptized anyone else. Notwithstanding this, he has a point to make and makes it clearly: 'Christ did not send me to baptize, but to proclaim the gospel.'

In the Acts of the Apostles we find just three references to Paul being involved with the act of baptizing. At Philippi, Lydia, a dealer in purple cloth, listened eagerly to Paul and was baptized, but we are not told if he himself baptized her (Acts 16.14–15). Also at Philippi, Paul and Silas were arrested. After an earthquake had shaken the prison in the night, they were released by the jailer who asked them how he might be saved, and that same night he and his family were baptized

(Acts 16.33). And then there were the disciples at Ephesus who had only received the baptism of John the Baptist and they were baptized in the name of Jesus (Acts 19.2–7). We are told that Paul laid his hands on them and that they received the Holy Spirit, but again we are not told if he himself baptized them.

Nevertheless, Paul is the great interpreter of baptism. He it is who sets out for us the meaning of this act of washing, and provides us with vivid imagery to illuminate the baptismal process. Baptism involves union with Christ. And in that union we are baptized into his death. Paul says quite categorically that we die with Christ. And the (ASB) baptism service reminds us that Jesus was brought through the deep waters of death and raised to life in triumph before it asks for a blessing on the water, that those washed in it 'may be made one with Christ in his death and in his resurrection to be cleansed and delivered from all sin'.

I wonder how seriously we take this, that we are made one with Christ and that this unity embraces both his death and his resurrection? Preaching in the mid-fifth century, Pope Leo the Great described baptism in this way: the renunciation of the devil and the affirmation of belief and trust in God, the passing from the old state into newness of life, the casting off of the earthly image, and the putting on of heavenly form – all this is a sort of dying and rising again, whereby the one who is received by Christ and who receives Christ is not the same after as before coming to the font. He says that the body of the regenerate – those who have passed through the water of baptism – becomes the flesh of the Crucified. *Corpus regenerati fiat caro crucifixi*. A closer union between Christ the Head and the members of his Body, the Church, can hardly be imagined.

'Christian, remember your dignity,' Pope Leo told a Christmas congregation,

> and now that you share in God's own nature, do not return by sin to your former base condition. Bear in mind who is your head and of whose body you are a member. Do not forget that you have been rescued from the power of darkness and brought into the light of God's kingdom. Through the sacrament of baptism you have become a temple of the Holy Spirit.

He is combining and drawing out the teaching that we find throughout the New Testament, that if we are in Christ, we are a new creation.

Surely we feel different if we say of ourselves, 'I am a new creation.' 'I am united to Christ.' 'I am a temple of the Holy Spirit.' 'I am not my own but Christ's.' What a dignity it gives us. Does it not make us want to stand taller, to act more boldly, to testify in word and deed to Christ who has conferred this upon us? Should it not also make us more resolute in resisting temptation and turning away from sin?

Paul was glad that he had baptized next to no one in Corinth because he did not want anyone to boast about being baptized by him. There was only one thing to boast of, only one thing worth boasting about – the grace and mercy of God in Christ. He wanted no one to forget that. Mark what he says. Have a good rummage and find your baptism certificate. Check the date. Write it on your calendar or in your diary. Mark it down as a significant anniversary, the day you became one with Christ, and let it stand year by year as a reminder so that you never forget that from that day on you were dead to sin and alive to God, in union with Christ Jesus.

THURSDAY OF THE FIRST WEEK:
Baptized into Christ's death

One Thursday in September 1994, I stood with my general practitioner at the side of the grave of a little girl, just five and a half months old. I had baptized her on 31 July. When we welcomed her into the Lord's family and affirmed that we were children of the same heavenly Father and inheritors together of the kingdom of God, we had no idea that she would enter so soon upon her inheritance. One week before the funeral she had returned with her parents from a holiday in Florida – a holiday amply recorded by video and still photographs. On Friday, she was ill. On Saturday, she died.

As I stood beside my GP in the churchyard of the parish of Sandhurst, the parish next door to mine where we buried our dead, I recalled that my last visit to the part of the churchyard where children are buried was a couple of years before for the funeral of another baby. The physician looked at the stone to which I had pointed. 'He was one of mine as well,' he said, and added, 'It is the one part of general practice for which I was not prepared.'

He was right, of course. The emphasis in medicine rests upon what the team of professionals, backed up by medical science and advanced technology, can do to maintain our health, to prevent illness wherever possible and to combat it when necessary. The target is a healthy life followed by an easy and relatively painless death. The death of a child is a failure; her small white coffin a reproach. Medicine – and by association her GP and mine – had let her down.

It fell to me not just to officiate at an unbelievably painful funeral service but also to try to aid the parents in making some sense of what had happened. No one expected me to heal her. They hadn't even thought to call me until she was dead. I could be considered a failure – and that again by association – only if God had failed them. Strangely perhaps, they didn't blame God. They didn't blame him because of an accidental or providential event: their little girl was born on Good Friday and in her parents' eyes she carried from the start the shadow of the cross and the hope of the resurrection. She was, they told me, she always would be, an Easter child.

We believe that Jesus, who opened wide his arms on the cross, put an end to death by dying for us and revealed the resurrection by rising to new life. Yet we may feel uncertain about what this means, this putting an end to death. I began by saying that a little child had died, and we ourselves expect to die. If we ignore that life-threatening collection – lightning and tempest, plague, pestilence and famine, battle and murder, and sudden death – then there must be sickness unto death from which we will not recover. We must come one day to the hour of our death and, firm in faith and fortified by the rites of the Church, we should welcome 'gentle Sister Death'.

There is a prayer in the Book of Common Prayer of 1662 to be said for a sick person, 'when there appeareth small hope of recovery'. It expresses a firm belief that God can even yet raise the sick person up but, given that the time of dissolution seems to draw near, it asks God to prepare the person against the hour of death that after his departure he may find peace and that his soul may be received into God's everlasting kingdom. In other words, it leaves the question of life or death to God and does what is necessary for the continuance of temporal life or the beginning of life everlasting.

But what is death if, by dying on the cross, Christ has put

an end to it? When that little girl was baptized, she was baptized into Christ's death. She was made one with Christ in
both his death and his resurrection. In consequence, death no
more had dominion over her. There will still be sickness and
dying until Christ is all in all, but we need not fear death. We
need not live as those without hope, and we see already some
of the benefits of Christ's Passion where faith receives them
and sin does not prevent their full efficacy.

FRIDAY OF THE FIRST WEEK:
A share in the work and joy of creation

Suffering is, nevertheless, one of those problems that comes round and round and provides a basic objection to religious belief. In a way, the Church has created the problem. In Sunday school I, like so many other children, was taught that we have a loving God who cares for us as a father cares for his children. This teaching went with a simplistic view of God sitting on a throne, wearing a long white robe, his bearded head surmounted by a golden crown. As a young curate I once shocked a congregation by asking, 'Does God wear underpants?' Children went home with glee to report that Mr Dudley had said the word 'underpants' during a service. It seemed a reasonable question – if God wears a long robe and sits on a throne, does he wear underpants? The absurdity of trying to answer it effectively undermined that picture of God.

I believe that we must have a clearer understanding of what creation means and so of the relation of the Creator to the creation. The world and our life in it is sustained by God. By the divine will, the creation is free. With the application of reason, we are able, to some extent, to determine how the creation develops. Our abuse of that freedom is part of what we call the fall. Freedom necessarily entails accepting the consequence of free actions. If we drive fast and recklessly and have a serious accident, angelic hands do not prevent it. If we climb a mountain and fall, a divine cushion does not appear to break the fall. God is not a divine version of International Rescue.

This is not the consequence of divine indifference. The

ASB baptism service, used when the little girl was baptized, reminded us that with the birth of children parents have a share in the work and joy of creation. The new born begins a perilous journey from babyhood to adulthood. Think of a child starting to walk. We recognize the possibility of injury, of the child falling on a hard or sharp surface. We know, however, that the child cannot be wrapped up in cotton wool and padding, not if he or she is to grow up to be a mature, autonomous, adult human being. If the child falls and is hurt, it is not because we are uncaring or unloving. We love the child even more in that moment, but we know that we must step back and give the child space to grow. The process of growing to maturity is a risky one and each stage of develop-ment has new risks.

The Creator steps back from the creation for the same reason. God loves what he has created and loves it more when he sees the turmoil, the pain and the anguish that freedom entails. Through the centuries, and particularly in the twentieth century, men and women have fought long and hard to estab-lish human freedom and human dignity and I do not believe we want our freedom taken away, even in the name of divine benevolence.

The Creator has stepped back from the creation but has by no means deserted it. His love is constantly made manifest and his goodness in sustaining the world is constantly evident. More than that, God has made it possible for us to enter into a relationship with him, characterized, as befits the relation of creature to Creator, by praise and worship. This relationship also allows for our prayer and intercession, for asking what is needful for ourselves, for others and for the common good. We are allowed, indeed encouraged, to address the Divine Majesty. Jesus assures us, when he teaches his disciples the

Our Father, that it is worth asking and persisting in asking. Though the Creator has allowed us a freedom which means that he does not, uninvited, interfere in our daily living, yet God is open to prayer and ready to receive intercession. This does not mean that, after prayer, our current problems will suddenly and inexplicably disappear. God often answers prayer in frankly unexpected ways. Yet if we are open to God and deliberately seek the divine will, we should expect that there will be a difference in our lives. That difference will not only be perceived at an inner, personal, spiritual level, but also in ways that affect our material well-being.

SATURDAY OF THE FIRST WEEK:
We do not see in the way God sees

We started the week with Noah. Tomorrow's eucharistic lections will bring us to Abraham, first known as Abram. Genesis is anxious to provide us with a genealogical link between Noah and Abram. Shem, Ham and Japheth, the sons of Noah, are themselves the fathers of all the nations that spread across the earth after the flood. Japheth was the father of the coastal peoples. Ham, the youngest son, was cursed by his father, and his descendants are those tribes that are later seen as enemies of Israel – Cush, Egypt and Canaan, and Canaan himself is the father of Sidon and of the Jebusites, the Amorites, the Girgashites, the Hivites, the Arkites, the Sinites, the Arvadites, the Zemarites and the Hamathites – the peoples who will be driven out of Canaan to allow the children of Israel to settle there. Shem also was father to many nations but it is his son Arpachshad who is the important one, for of his line is born Terah, father of Abram, Nahor and Haran. This myth of origins is important. Babel explains the diversity of languages; this genealogical table explains the origins of diverse peoples and also explains why some – the sons of Ham – were not pleasing to God.

But a further strand emerges from it – that of the chosen ones to whom the promise is given and who act in faith. This strand goes against the logic of power. It is not the most powerful who are chosen by God. This is not some version of evolution, of the survival of the fittest. This is about the sovereign power of God. In a way, therefore, it is about how God is, by our standards, by our judgement, unreasonable.

There seems to be no logic in his choice or reason in his acts of rejection. Abel is preferred to Cain, Noah is favoured over all other people; Shem and Japheth are blessed and Ham and his son Canaan are cursed; Arpachshad is chosen from among the children of Shem and Abram from among the children of Nahor. And Abram is chosen despite the barrenness of his wife Sarai, indeed because of it. We are not asked to judge God; we are not able to do so. We do not see in the way God sees. Human hearts are not open to us but to the Creator they are all open. We see the present, ponder the past, plan for the future. All time, all ages are present to God. There is a deeper logic than the one we are capable of understanding, a logic which brings into co-operative union the sovereign freedom of God and human beings in their God-given freedom. So perhaps the divine choice rests on those who will agree, who will accept the divine will, from Noah to the Blessed Virgin Mary, from Abraham to the Apostle Paul. There is here a sort of counter logic that has appealed to the theologians of liberation, a choice that seems deliberately to rest upon the humble and meek, that seems deliberately to put down the mighty from their seats. God chooses the barren, when barrenness was a sign of the divine curse; the poor, when wealth is seen as an indicator of divine favour; he chooses women in a patriarchal society, and the outcast of society as the prophetic voice. In other words, there is a strong undercurrent in the divine disorder that opposes the prevailing order of majesty, power and might.

SECOND SUNDAY OF LENT:
Out of Egypt have I called my son

For us to understand the covenant with Abram and what it means for us, we must take a little time to follow the stories of Israel's patriarchs. In Genesis 12 we have the first major appearance of Egypt in the Bible. In Genesis 10 it was said that Egypt was one of the sons of Ham, the youngest son of Noah, the one who was cursed. But the Egypt that we next encounter is clearly a highly developed country under its ruler, the Pharaoh, and perhaps more importantly it is a country generally free from famine because of the annual Nile flood which enriches the fields. It is also a country of strange gods, a country imbued with mystery and magic. For the writer of the kabbalistic Zohar, Egypt represents the dark underside of wisdom; the journey, the descent into Egypt – the biblical traveller always goes *down* into Egypt – is both necessary and dangerous. It is part of the pilgrimage, part of the journey of transformation. Abram will go down into Egypt and return. His is an individual journey. Israel goes down into Egypt and that is both an individual journey and a corporate one. Out of the experience of being in Egypt the chosen people Israel is shaped and formed. Though some do not return from the descent, others are formed by it as in a crucible. Moses, born in Egypt and initiated into all the secrets of the Egyptians, will leave and return to Egypt, and then leave again reformed. It is, therefore, not surprising that Jesus the Messiah also goes down into Egypt to fulfil the prophecy, 'Out of Egypt have I called my son' (Hosea 11.1; Matthew 2.15).

Two realities are represented by Egypt. First, a place. A developed culture as opposed to the inchoate forms of Hebraic life. A settled society in urban communities along the Nile. Builders in stone. A people united under a ruler. Second, a spiritual realm where temptations and deceptions abound, a realm of temples, initiations and initiates, with a developed fertility religion based on the dying and rising of Osiris. Not the least of these temptations and paths to wisdom was sexual. Egyptian religion honoured a number of female deities, not least Isis, and a powerful reverence for sexual fecundity permeated religious practice.

Abram, therefore, descends into Egypt, driven there by famine, and he takes Sarai with him. Now these few verses of Genesis 12 in which Abram deceives the Egyptians, lying to them in order to save his life, and putting Sarai at some risk, have a curiously contemporary ring to them. Here is the man who will be venerated as the father of many nations, the one to whom God's promises are made and in whom they are fulfilled, and he is guilty of perjury, obstruction of justice, tampering with witnesses – for he must have told the rest of the family to support his version of things – and abuse of power, for it is the Egyptians who suffer because of Abram's deception. The only thing that is clear when dealing with issues of morality is that nothing is ever clear-cut. We might say, in Abram's defence, that there is a strong Middle Eastern tradition of deception, of things not being what they seem to be, and this has sometimes confused the straightforward European mind!

Abram is very matter-of-fact. Sarai is beautiful. The Egyptians like beautiful women. If they know he is her husband, they will kill him and take her. So let her be thought of as his sister, and they will court her and reward him. And that is exactly what happens. Abram receives sheep, oxen, asses, camels, menservants and maidservants, and Sarai is taken into Pharaoh's household. More than that, Pharaoh unwittingly takes her to be his wife. Let us be quite clear about this: Pharaoh innocently enters upon a sexual relationship with Sarai and that is the reason why he and his household are afflicted with plagues. I think that we would want to say that this was Abram's fault and his alone. As soon as Pharaoh learns what has happened, he returns Sarai to Abram and sends him packing. Abram has been enriched in the process; we are not told what Sarai thought about it.

There is also no judgement against Abram in Genesis. Many of the leaders of Israel will be castigated in Scripture – Moses for speaking in haste as if he were God; Samson for his taste in women; Eli for his inability to control his sons; David for the seduction of Bathsheba, for the murder of Uriah, for ordering a census; Solomon for embracing the gods of his wives. Of Abram there is no criticism, and there emerges from the pages of Genesis a complex character, oddly trusting and obedient on the one hand, and cunning and duplicitous on the other. An early example of being as wise as a serpent and as innocent as a dove.

Do we see anything here from which we can learn, apart from a further affirmation that the sovereign will of God confuses human logic and favours those whom we might presume to reject? Yes, there is the matter of the descent into Egypt and our own spiritual and psychological journey. The Egyptians knew that, in order to pass through the underworld, you needed magic texts, you needed to know the names of the guardians of the portals, you needed to confuse and deceive those who would obstruct your passage. Abram is here depicted as one who, by a means that we may not applaud, passed through and came out of Egypt. The religious tradition of the West needs neither Eastern spirituality nor psychological insight, for it knows already of the light and dark sides of wisdom. Wisdom, in its dark side, represented by alchemy and magic, contains the possibility of use, or rather abuse, in that we gain power over others and use it to our short-term advantage. The dark side of wisdom is bewitching, charming, in the literal sense of those words. It brings no long-term gain but when we realize its power we may be seduced by it. If we do not enter into knowledge of it, going, spiritually and psychologically, down into Egypt, then we will always remain ignorant both of it and of the higher levels of spiritual development. It is the crucible that changes us.

MONDAY OF THE SECOND WEEK:
I will make your descendants as the dust of the earth

When Abram came up out of Egypt he was very rich – rich in cattle but also in silver and in gold. Yet he still dwelt in tents and moved frequently to new pasture. His was a peripatetic existence. And so he again came to the place, between Bethel on the west and Ai on the east, where he had first made an altar and there, we are told, Abram called on the Lord. We may presume that he made a sacrifice. It is not explicitly stated that he did but perhaps the precise language of sacrifice was deliberately omitted by the priestly editor because you could not have sacrifice until there were priests and there were no priests as yet in Abram's day!

It was after he had called on the name of the Lord that he made a decision. Perhaps, more than sacrifice, Abram was engaged in an act of divination, of perceiving the divine will for himself. Certainly there are numerous occasions in the early books of the Old Testament when people sought by many different means to know what they should do in this or that situation. Such requests for knowledge come close to magic and often involve looking for certain confirmatory signs of a preferred activity. After this consultation, Abram spoke to Lot. Lot was Abram's nephew, the son of his brother Haran, who had predeceased their father. Perhaps that was why Lot was with Abram, because his own father was dead. Together, however, it was difficult to find pasture. There were simply too many animals and there was always a danger of strife between the herdsmen. So Abram puts to Lot a proposal that they should now divide into two groups – Lot and his family and herds going one way and Abram going another – and Abram allows Lot to make the choice.

Looked at with hindsight, this is a further stage in the shaping of Abram as the father of many nations. It also reveals a tension that is evident throughout Israel's history, between the peripatetic life of the herdsman and the settled life of the city dweller. The former is seen as purer, as closer to God. We will see it when David is called from the sheepfolds to be king over Israel, and we will see it in the tidal flow between Jerusalem and the countryside and the wilderness in the life and ministry of Jesus. Lot's choice is the wrong one. He chooses the fertile valley of the Jordan where there were cities, and the greatest of the cities were Sodom and Gomorrah, and the men of Sodom were wicked, great sinners against the Lord.

Abram makes the right choice, seeking not his own gain but the will of God, and that will is now expressed in God's promise to Abram. The first stage of the promise came when Abram left his father's house and was told, 'I will make of you a great nation, and I will bless you and make your name great ... and in you all the families of the earth shall be blessed' (Genesis 12.2–3). Now the promise is specifically linked to the land which will be given to Abram's descendants, though as yet he has none. Yet God promises: 'I will make your offspring like the dust of the earth; so that if one can count the dust of the earth, your offspring also can be counted' (Genesis 13.16).

So, says Genesis, as a consequence of this promise, Abram moved his tents until he came to the oaks of Mamre, at Hebron. The scene is therefore set for a series of encounters with God which turn Abram son of Terah into Abraham, father of Isaac, grandfather of Jacob, whom God called Israel.

The process we are witnessing is one of spiritual transformation. It is not a matter-of-fact experience. It is not one that we shall easily understand and some of the details of it will perplex us. That is the nature of spiritual change and as God does not change so the nature of mystical experience contains certain constant features. We can learn from Abram's experience what our own is or might be like when we trust in the promises of God.

TUESDAY OF THE SECOND WEEK:
Is anything too hard for the Lord?

In Genesis 17, God gave Abram and Sarai new names, calling them Abraham and Sarah. Their new names marked a transition in their lives as God renewed his promise to Abraham and moved to fulfil it. Abraham had long been promised that he would be the father of countless descendants but had begotten only Ishmael by Sarah's maidservant Hagar. Now Sarah is promised a son. Three men came one summer to the tents by the oaks of Mamre and received Abraham's hospitality. Those three men, who will subsequently be seen as an expression of the Trinity, promised to return in the spring when Sarah, now of great age, would have a son. Hidden by the tent flap, Sarah laughed, and the messenger expressed surprise, asking, 'Why did Sarah laugh? Is anything too hard for the Lord?'

There was a movement in the 1960s and 1970s that approached the text of the Bible, and especially of the Gospels and Acts, with a complete rejection of miracles. The view rested on a philosophical position which would not accept the possibility of miraculous intervention in a world ordered by laws discovered by science – for a miracle, by definition, violated these laws. Healing miracles could be explained in terms of psychology but children born to the aged and infertile, the sea turned back, the sun standing still in its course, the turning of water into wine, walking on the sea, and the feeding of crowds with a few loaves and fish were, simply, straightforwardly, impossible. They were – it was argued – the product of a different culture, a culture that accepted miracles uncritically.

Today we seem to have an equally uncritical acceptance of the miraculous among certain groups within the Christian Church and a strong desire for such miracles outside the Church. If the former attitude clung too strongly to scientific values, the latter seems unable to cope with a scientific view. Millennial fever has intensified this irrationalism and the anti-scientific approach is most obviously seen in the idea among some American evangelicals that the so-called millennium bug is God's judgement on the world, in the same way that AIDS was considered by them to be divine judgement on the prevailing approach to human sexuality. Such an apocalyptic vision of the world is not a necessary result of Christian faith.

The liturgy provides a surer guide to the interaction of the divine and human, the spiritual and the material, for it demonstrates the constant interaction between them. The material world has its origin in God and is sustained by the divine will, but it has its own characteristics, its own freedom, its own laws. The liturgy stresses outward and visible material things as signs of inward and spiritual graces. In other words, the material world – as the Apostle Paul says in Romans 1 – reveals the presence of God, but also and more specifically shows God's love for and action towards us.

This action is sometimes marked by those actions that we term miraculous, actions that go beyond our expectations, that move to the very edges of what is possible, to the limits of the natural world. Science can deal only with events that can be repeated, measured, and repeated again. God's one-off actions defy such measurement and repetition. They are not assured. They cannot be ordered. The divine will remains sovereign and cannot be manipulated. But we are given the means to be open to the power of God, means focused in and consolidated by the liturgy and the celebration of the sacraments.

I hold to a middle position – one that affirms the sovereignty of God and the freedom of the creation but also affirms the possibility that, for us and for our salvation, God will use his power. And further that such use of power is, in the Church, mediated through prayer and the sacraments. Nothing is too hard for the Lord.

WEDNESDAY OF THE SECOND WEEK:
A faith like Abraham's

There was a collect in the Alternative Service Book that was used seven Sundays before Christmas. It concerned Abraham and described him as faithfully obeying God's call and rejoicing in the promise that all the families of the earth would be blessed in him. It then asked, 'Give us a faith like his, that, in us, your promises might be fulfilled.' The lesson in the first year was the call to Abram to leave his native land, but in the second year it was the story in Genesis 22 in which God calls upon Abraham to take his son, his only son, whom he loved, and to offer him in sacrifice. This lesson, like that of Noah and the flood, had been included in the Easter Vigil readings, before Pope Pius XII's reform of the Roman rite in the 1950s. The Gospel provides a context in which the story of Isaac is seen as a type of the sacrifice of Christ, but without such a context I have always found it grotesque and felt that the very last thing I would want is a blind faith like Abraham's, an unquestioning obedience to the will of God.

This passage perhaps more than any other points to a tension between divine sovereignty and human freedom, between the will of the Creator and the liberty of the creation. There are people who reject their freedom, who want to hand it over to some higher authority, human or divine or the human that is made quasi-divine, like the Grand Inquisitor in Dostoevesky's *The Brothers Karamazov*. There are also those who want others to determine what they believe – this, said the Spanish writer Unamuno, is the faith of the charcoal-burner. If you ask him what he believes, he tells you to ask the priest; he knows what the charcoal-burner believes and whatever the priest says, he believes it. It may seem simpler to have a faith like Abraham's but I have always preferred to be like the Apostle Thomas: to be hesitant, to be prepared to doubt, for doubt is only a preamble to faith. I do not see how we can prefer blind faith when so many today rush blindly into the fundamentalisms that bind will and intellect and subscribe to personal revelations that go beyond Scripture to provide apparently authoritative teaching about the situation of Christians in the world today.

There is no expectation in Christianity that we will surrender the use of our intellect and our critical skills. Our faith is not a blind one. Rather we are, by prayer, by meditation on Scripture, by our participation in worship and our reception of the sacraments, to learn to see with the eye of faith, to use the vision that sees God at work in the world and co-operates with that work. God does not destroy our human nature, but perfects it. God does not overpower our will and undermine our intellect but facilitates their use in faith. It might be easier to have a faith like Abraham's; I have never felt able to ask for it.

THURSDAY OF THE SECOND WEEK:
I am God Almighty, El Shaddai

Isaac, as we know, was not sacrificed. God substituted a ram and Isaac went on to be married to Rebekah who was the mother of Esau and Jacob. The stories of these patriarchs – Abraham, Isaac and Jacob – take up the chapters from Genesis 12 until Genesis 50. They are marvellous stories, rich in imagery, demonstrating the calling of God's chosen people. Here we can read of the way Jacob cheated Esau out of his inheritance, how he dreamed of a ladder set up between earth and heaven and received the promise God had made to Abraham, and of how he loved Rachel and worked for fourteen years to have her as his wife. And the story of Jacob, now called Israel, leads into the story of his sons and especially of Joseph.

Joseph precedes his brothers and sets the scene for Israel's bondage in Egypt. The great saga that begins with the stories of Joseph and ends with the Exodus is the really crucial story without which the rest of Scripture makes little sense. As the whole story is a long one we tend, when we read it in church, to break it up into manageable portions and so lose sight of the whole. The Joseph-cycle tells how Joseph of the many-coloured coat was sold into slavery by his brothers but, by divine providence, became deputy to Pharaoh, King of Egypt, in the years of plenty and of famine foretold by dreams. It tells how Joseph welcomed to Egypt his father Israel and all his family and his flocks and herds. The Book of Genesis concludes with the death of Joseph, and his body being embalmed after the manner of the Egyptians and placed in a coffin in Egypt.

Genesis is the great book of beginnings that attempts to explain through myth and story the origins of human diversity and the multiplicity of languages, and to explain death, the meaning of labour and the source of human sexual desire. It is one of the richest of books and repays careful reading and rereading. As Christians we read it, without apology, through the lenses and filters provided by the New Testament. We hear Paul's verdict on this or that character and see them held up in Hebrews as those who acted in faith. We see, as well, that faith is not merely blind trust, that it does not carry success always, that the will of God for us may be unfolded only in time, and that what we call accident and coincidence can as easily serve the divine will as that which is deliberately willed and carefully planned. Genesis constantly reminds us that the divine will is unfathomable but that God remains true to his word and fulfils his promises.

FRIDAY OF THE SECOND WEEK:
The bondage of the human soul

Exodus opens with the descendants of Israel being fruitful and multiplying and with the ominous words, 'Now there arose a new king over Egypt, who did not know Joseph' (Exodus 1.8, RSV). These words set the scene for the opposition between the Egyptians – civilized city dwellers, warriors and administrators – and the Israelites, the keepers of flocks and herds like their forebears. We cannot be entirely clear how the biblical narrative fits with what we know of Egyptian history, but we do have sufficient evidence of similar conflicts to recognize that this one belongs to a familiar historical pattern. The Bible is little concerned with dates and dynasties. It sets down the history of salvation, the relationship between God and the chosen people.

We often find that, as we read history, we support one side rather than the other: Romans against barbarians, Alfred against the Danes, Anglo-Saxons against Normans. The Egyptian-Israelite conflict depicted in Scripture creates a few problems for me. I have loved the Egyptians and their civilization since I first looked at mummy cases in Birmingham Museum and Art Gallery as a child (and I preferred Yul Brynner to Charlton Heston in *The Ten Commandments*), so I find it quite hard to accept them as the villains of this story. Nevertheless, Exodus depicts them as hard taskmasters laying heavy burdens on the Israelites, and the cry of his people is heard by God, the God of Abraham, Isaac and Jacob.

In Exodus 4, Moses encounters God in the burning bush and he is given the commission to lead Israel out of Egypt.

In the conflict that follows God seems to be playing both sides, urging Moses on *and* hardening Pharaoh's heart. God is preparing Israel for a manifestation of his power and the intensification of the struggle is a necessary prelude to it.

The captivity in Egypt can also be read allegorically as the bondage of the human soul enslaved by sin. This reading of Exodus is not simple or straightforward. Israel was not in bondage because it chose to be, but because that which was perceived as good – the refuge in Egypt from the famine – became enslavement. Though the Israelites complained vigorously about it, they could tolerate it, and their anger was turned against Moses and Aaron when their attempt to release them led to still greater burdens. The attempt to break out of bondage becomes an intensification of the bondage, and a greater struggle is needed before there can be release. So we too can become dependent on that which, being neither good nor bad in itself, comes to enslave us. We live with that enslavement. We accommodate ourselves to our bondage, become used to our limitations, and hardly notice the erosion of our freedom. Failed attempts to be free of the bondage of sin are like attempts to break out of addiction; they can force us into deeper dependence until the ultimate crisis, the passing over from death to life. This pattern of enslavement and release is to be found deeply embedded in our human history, corporate and personal. Israel's salvation history is our history and that is why we need to attend to it.

SATURDAY OF THE SECOND WEEK:
Let my people go

El Shaddai, the Great I AM, the Lord God Almighty, says to Moses, 'Go into Pharaoh, King of Egypt, and tell him, let my people go.' And there is more: God tells Moses, 'Say to the people of Israel, thus says God, I am the Lord, and I will bring you out from under the burdens of the Egyptians.' These are no small tasks that Moses is given, and he knows it. He had tried already to take the Israelites out into the desert to offer sacrifice. That request had been refused. The Egyptians saw it as an attempt to avoid hard labour and the Israelites were punished by being forced to gather the straw they needed before they could make the daily quota of bricks. Moses' first attempt met with failure and brought down upon him the scorn and derision of the Israelites. And Moses has to appear before the King of Upper and Lower Egypt, crowned with the cobra and the vulture, descendent of Amun-Re, the sun-god, and demand in the name of the God of Abraham, Isaac and Jacob that his people might go free.

As the story unfolds God continues to play both sides – encouraging Moses and hardening Pharaoh's heart. We need to recognize that what is planned here is a mighty victory, an awesome display of divine power, an act of such majesty that the gods of the Egyptians will be seen as empty, powerless idols. The chosen people will know who is their God and be bound to him for ever. An easy victory is of no use. It will not accomplish this.

And so the struggle begins. Pharaoh is not impressed by conjuring tricks with snakes. The magicians of Egypt, by their secret arts, could do the same as Moses and Aaron. Nor is Pharaoh persuaded when the Nile is turned to blood, for his magicians could do that as well. And the plague of frogs was hardly more remarkable, for that, too, was performed by the magicians. Even when Moses and Aaron brought up gnats from the dust and the magicians, unable to duplicate this, said, 'This is the finger of God', Pharaoh was not ready to give in. And though the plague of flies, and the plague on the cattle, horses, asses, camels and herds, and the boils, and the hail, and the locusts weakened Pharaoh's resolve, yet each time his heart was again hardened and he refused to let Israel go. When darkness fell on the land, Pharaoh relented: Israel could go, but not the flocks and herds. Moses would not accept this. Israel needed sacrificial offerings for the Lord and they could not go without them, and so they remained.

After this Pharaoh dismissed Moses from his presence and said, 'Get away from me; take heed to yourself; never see my face again; for in the day you see my face you shall die' (Exodus 10.28, RSV). And so the Lord, the God of Israel, came to the last of the wonders he would work against Egypt – the death of the firstborn, from the death of Pharaoh's son to the death of the miller's daughter's son. That night, the night in which the Lord went forth in the midst of Egypt, was the night of Passover: the night of the sacrificial lamb eaten in haste, the night of watching for the Lord, the night when the bonds of the Israelites were broken. On that night the Israelites, their flocks and their herds, went out of Egypt and despoiled the Egyptians.

This story, once so well known and now so neglected, provides a crucial strand for our understanding of the Passion of Christ. Israel's bondage is the type and symbol of human bondage, of our subjection to sin which, rather than being a delight, reduces and even eliminates our freedom. Passover was the night of watching for the Lord, the night of the Lord's power. Good Friday, in a remarkable reversal, sees the death of the only begotten Son of God. Holy Saturday night, that most holy of all nights, sees death conquered rather than death as the means of conquest, and brings about the end of the bondage of sin.

Ritual, myth, allegory and metaphor do not easily translate into propositions to be believed. Poetry and story embody the truth more readily than doctrinal statements do. The liturgy of Lent, Holy Week and Easter is not made up of a series of lectures or discursive explorations of salvation. It is a ritualized acting out, a sacramental expression. We cannot suspend the rational faculties when dealing with faith, but we have to nurture other senses, the ones we use to appreciate drama and music, architecture, painting and sculpture.

THIRD SUNDAY OF LENT:
Bless me, for I have sinned

During Lent 1992 I was in the United States. I went to make my confession. That was not unusual. What was unusual was that it was not my regular confessor. He was in Bath and I was in Cambridge, Massachusetts. So I went to the Cowley Fathers. Snow had fallen overnight and was still falling as I walked from the Episcopal Divinity School to the monastery. It looked more beautiful than ever, a timeless expression of Christian simplicity beside the river.

The priest who saw me did not know me already, so we sat for a while talking. It was very pleasant. An enjoyable conversation. Only a cup of tea would have made it more pleasant. I explained who I was and what I was doing in America. He spoke of how the Fathers had all been to England in 1991.

When the change came, it was a small thing, barely noticeable. We still sat there as before. His purple stole was one of those short, ribbon-like ones. I was briefly reminded of Mulcahey in *M*A*S*H*, and then I said, 'Bless me, Father, for I have sinned.'

Bless me, for I have sinned. It is the traditional, time-honoured beginning of a confession. It is so different from an apology to a friend that begins in sorrow, so different from giving oneself up to arrest, trial, judgement and punishment. It is a simple, eloquent statement of the human predicament: bless me, for I have sinned. Because I have sinned I am in greater need of that blessing. Bless me, because I need grace, I need help, I need confidence, I need the gifts of truth and humility if I am to confess, if my lips are to overcome the reticence of shame and the fear of disapproval, if they are to utter words which I would prefer to leave unspoken. Bless me, for I have sinned, and without your blessing I can go no further.

It is easier when we say together 'we confess that we have sinned'. Solidarity in sin is such a relief, because I feel certain that my sins will get mixed up with yours and pass unnoticed in the general confession. It is *our* fault and *we* are sorry. That solidarity doesn't uphold me when I say 'I have sinned', and admit that it was *my* fault, my own deliberate fault. It does not uphold me when I acknowledge that there are not only sins that I can remember but, worse still, sins that I have forgotten. Can I really be living in such a daze that I don't remember committing sins?

MONDAY OF THE THIRD WEEK:
Allow yourself to be forgiven

In uptown Manhattan, at the corner of Broadway and 155th Street, is a remarkable edifice, the Church of the Intercession which was for many years a daughter church to Trinity, Wall Street. It is a remarkable and unexpected complex of build- ings erected on Audubon's farm and set in the middle of a cemetery. In its crypt there is a Chapel of the Resurrection. It was the first columbarium provided in New York, and the chapel is today home to a congregation of Mar Thoma Christians from India. Their worship is in Malayalam for three Sundays of the month and in English once. The English book, which I picked up, contains this confession:

> We confess to you, Lord, what we are:
> We are not the people we like others to think we are;
> We are afraid to admit even to ourselves what lies
>   in the depths of our souls,
> But we do not want to hide our true selves from you.
>
> We believe that you know us as we are, and yet you
>   love us.
> Help us not to shrink from self-knowledge;
> teach us to respect ourselves for your sake;
> give us courage to put our trust in your guiding power.

There could be no more eloquent statement of the reasons why we make confession of our sin. It is love that drives us, love that beckons us. To allow ourselves to be forgiven is to allow ourselves to be loved.

When my elder son was a small boy of three years of age and had fallen out with me, he would sometimes come into my study, all by himself, without any prompting, and say to me, 'I'm sorry, Daddy. I won't do it again.' He would put his arms out for comfort, for consolation, for forgiveness, for love, and my anger would go from me and my heart melt and my eyes would often fill with tears. If a human father will behave in such a way, how much greater must be the consolation we receive from our heavenly Father? When I consider the way in which unresolved hurt has caused a barrier at various times between me and other people – my parents, my wife, one or other friend, parishioners – I see that this is the only way forward. The alternative, all too often, is the scowl, the ominous silence, and the constant attempt to avoid those we have hurt. We must persevere in resisting evil and whenever we fall into sin, repent and return to the Lord.

Here, again, it must be said that it isn't easy and that is why we begin by asking for a blessing. Paul reminds us of the fundamental truth that the temptation that seizes us is common to all humanity. 'I am the worst of sinners,' a lady declared at a revivalist meeting. 'Do not delude yourself,' replied the preacher. The call to repentance is not a slap in the face. It reminds us of our human tendency to succumb to temptation and calls us to do something about it; to resist where we can and to repent when we succumb.

You may never have made your confession. When I did for the first time, as a convert from the Baptist Church to an Anglo-Catholicism already in crisis, I did so because it was the catholic thing to do. I wanted to belong, to be part of the catholic whole. It took some time before I went to confession because of God's love for me and my love for God, before I grasped its true value and its absolute simplicity. I cannot say that I ever enjoy doing it and there are prolonged periods when I eschew it until the gospel again summons me to seek reconciliation. As you examine your life and faith and witness this Lent you might find it useful for your growth.

Confession rarely takes long — less time than you spend in the dentist's chair! Almost the last thing the priest says is this: 'The Lord has put away all your sins.' It seems remarkable, doesn't it? One minute I am saying, 'I have sinned' and before very long those sins which were such an intolerable burden, so difficult to name and impossible to justify, are gone, put away by the Lord, never to be brought out again. And so we can go on in peace.

TUESDAY OF THE THIRD WEEK:
Manifold sins and wickedness

Confession today is, however, rather complicated. The question is, 'What shall we confess?' Or, to turn it round, how shall we determine what is right? How shall we know what is our duty? How do we identify that which is good? These are perennial questions. They did not arrive with Christianity nor even with the faith of Israel. They are questions fully developed in the writings of Plato, who died in 347 BC, and of his younger contemporary, Aristotle.

Throughout Plato's Socratic dialogues – those that have Plato's teacher Socrates as the principal speaker – there is a deep concern with virtue and whether it can be taught, and this concern extends into the *Protagoras*, where the nature of the good is discussed and into Plato's supreme creation, *The Republic*, in which he examines the nature of right conduct and of the ideal political state. Plato speaks with passion, as we rarely do these days, of goodness, truth, and beauty and of the cultivation of the mind and the achievement of true insight. One can hardly summarize Plato in a line but he believes, fervently believes, that the soul naturally aims at what it believes to be good and that wrongdoing is the pursuit of what is falsely considered to be good. The key, therefore, to goodness is knowledge, and this means not an accumulation of facts or laws, not an arid cerebral knowing, but a knowledge of the good that engages the entirety of what we are. This apprehension of the nature of what is good is very different from one that is derived from sets of rules and lists of commandments.

I suppose that I bought my copy of *A Simple Prayer Book* in the early 1970s. It was price 1s but underneath, in brackets, it says 5p – so that dates it fairly easily. It came from the Catholic Truth Society. It had been first published in 1886 and this edition was revised after the Second Vatican Council and carried the imprimatur of Cardinal Heenan. It was a useful little book for one who knew nothing of Roman Catholicism, but it was also rather perplexing. Five pages are taken up with confession. There are prayers to be said before, including one in which the penitent, preparing for confession, asks God, 'Give me light to see what sins I have committed since my last confession.' The penitent is then reminded of an obligation to confess all mortal sins and guided in the examination of conscience.

This examination is a key part of the traditional practice of confession. It is not just a listing of transgressions but a genuine enquiry into the reasons why the person has failed to keep the commandments of God and the Church, failed in perfection, and sinned directly or indirectly against God. But what follows is a list of questions, carefully phrased so that innocent minds might not be prompted to sin. There are too many to list here but two or three will give the flavour: Have I been careless in my preparation for, or thanksgiving after receiving the sacraments? Have I revealed the faults of others in idle gossip? Have I contributed to the support of the Church in proportion to my means? Have I brooded over injuries, or refused to forgive? After this examination of conscience there were acts of contrition, the form for confession and absolution, and finally a thanksgiving.

We have here, just as much as in Plato, a fully defined and entirely practical approach to perceiving what is right and avoiding what is wrong. But where Plato talks of goodness, truth and beauty, and their negation in what is evil, the catholic tradition uses the language of sin, penitence, confession and forgiveness. And our own Anglican strand long maintained in its inheritance from the Middle Ages the language of erring and straying, of offending against God's laws, of manifold sins and wickedness, of intolerable burdens. And though we may be unaware of it, we are also exhorted by the Prayer Book to search and examine our consciences before receiving Holy Communion, to examine our lives and conversations by the rule of God's commandments and, in case of offence, to confess to Almighty God, with full purpose of amendment of life. The Roman Catholic mechanism of confession may have been more highly elaborated but it is basically the same in intent and purpose as that to which the Anglican tradition calls us.

It is not just the religious tradition that shapes our thinking about right and wrong. Nor is it Plato, at least not directly. Our needs and aspirations, our tendencies and desires, have been thoroughly analysed by philosophy and psychology, by social and behavioural sciences. The media espouse a variety of positions on what makes for the *good life* and how, usually by conspicuous consumption, we can achieve it. And within this approach or series of approaches, everything is of the same value: going to church and playing tennis, exploring the street markets and going to the cinema. Those who work with selfless devotion for charitable causes are held up for admiration but so are the media stars of soap operas and chat shows. In this absence of hierarchy, of ordering according to that which serves goodness, truth and beauty, the Christian principle of sin, even when residual and no longer connected to active belief, trips in at the last like some safety device, finally and hopelessly declaring that something is wrong.

That is a very long way from Plato's intention to promote what is good and not merely to indicate what is bad. It turns things upside down. It makes Christianity a religion primarily concerned with sin, guilt and penance. It magnifies the dark side without increasing the light. And we can see that happening in both public and private life with the need to define standards not by indicating what we should be striving for but primarily by indicating what we should avoid. That is surely not what we are about. What is held up before us in the wonder of creation and the mystery of love is something that defines our redeemed humanity in terms of its dignity, not its failings; its potential, not its limitations; its glory, not its shame. Dust returning to dust, but so much more than that as well.

It may be, quite simply, that we have for too long accepted a moral relativism in which each approach offered to us is put in a separate box within and we open that box and use that set of tools depending on whether we are concerned with business, education, recreation, sexuality, medical matters, culture high and low. What we lack is an integrating principle, some vision that makes sense of and orders our lives without suppressing our freedom. It cannot be bought off the shelf nor acquired for 1s. And we will only find it if we look for it and look not just privately and personally – for we know that morality has a public face – but by conversing, discussing, reading, thinking, praying together, in search of all that is good and true and beautiful.

THURSDAY OF THE THIRD WEEK:
The evocation of beauty

Less than ten years after the end of the Second World War, a publishing house in Frankfurt am Main produced a lavishly illustrated ten-volume introduction to the German lands – a celebration of its natural beauty, its architectural glories, and its rich and varied history. I have several of these books acquired piecemeal from second-hand bookshops and each of them is a delight. They succeed in their avowed intention of turning the reader's thoughts away from the disaster of recent events, away from the evil memory of the Nazi years. Much the same was done by another book, *Heritage of Beauty: Architecture and Sculpture in Austria*, described on the cover as of 'pleasant evocative power' catching the 'real old Austria which an Austrian can accept as authentic'.

The evocation of beauty is an antidote to the gloom, filth and death which seem to be so popular in art today. We must not be ashamed of beauty because it takes our minds away from inhumanity as well as distracting us from the trivial, banal aspects of daily living. Beauty is an important and neglected aspect of our humanity and a necessary source of nourishment for the soul. It is not an escape from reality, for that which is beautiful is as real as that which is ugly, evil and life-denying. Beauty lies in the complex interrelation of light and form, in colour, shape and texture, but also in the way we see, in the eye of the beholder.

The medieval mind set the ugly, the deformed and the unnatural against beauty, perfection and nature redeemed by grace. This was done most simply and effectively by painting a judgement, dividing the saved and the damned, contrasting devils and angels. This is an attractive and effective method of illustrating difference, but it is not a truthful method. Except for a very few rare individuals — the obviously saintly and the unequivocally wicked — we, the vast majority of human beings, are an admixture, combining in varying proportions features of both extremes and of all that lies between. We are not the black souls destined for hell or those robed in unspotted garments who stand before the throne.

FRIDAY OF THE THIRD WEEK:
The way of life and peace

In order to live the Christian life, that is to live daily as disciples of Christ following him to Jerusalem, we need a good deal of realism. This realism enables us to rejoice at the beauty of life without scruple or reservation and to acknowledge failure and sinfulness without neurosis or despair. We need to acknowledge that we are dust returning to dust, certainly, but we need also to know that we are more than that, a redeemed humanity. We can learn something from those Austrian and German volumes. They were in German and intended for a German readership. It was necessary to set before the readers who had so recently experienced defeat, humiliation and shame, an image of beauty to help them recover some sense of pride, a pride that would lead to reconstruction of their country and society based on the best principles. In a rather similar way, at what I believe is the end of a very difficult period in the history of the Church, we need to hold before our eyes the beauty of our religious inheritance, its strengths, its achievements, its delights. It is easy to feel bad about it all and so much more difficult to feel good. We need an evocation of the Christian tradition and specifically our Anglican tradition that we recognize as authentic and which will inspire us.

This is not without its problems. It could be objected that the series *Die Deutsche Lande* in depicting traditional Germany portrayed the very seedbed from which Nazism arose – a Germanic superiority expressed in buildings and monuments and an Aryan folk culture. And a portrayal of our inheritance might also be a tribute to effortless Anglican superiority which has marked so much of our history and especially our relations with other Christians. Beauty is not flawless. Tradition is not all good. Yet even with these reservations, the frank recognition of wheat and tares growing together, I would rather that we celebrated the beauty of our religion, the beauty of salvation, the beauty of holiness, lifting our eyes toward heaven rather than wallowing in a mire of sinfulness and failure.

This is a good moment to recognize this, for we are more than halfway through Lent, almost on the eve of Laetare or Refreshment Sunday. We may need to lift our hearts and eyes up from the dust because, once we get a grip on it, we are much better at sackcloth and ashes than we are at festal garments! Christianity needs to be concerned about sin but it is not primarily, or even mostly, about sin and judgement. It is about life and wholeness. The way of the cross is none other than the way of life and peace.

SATURDAY OF THE THIRD WEEK:
A merry heart doeth good like a medicine

A few years ago I had a mailing from an insurance company. It urged me to make provision for the unexpected events of life by taking out various types of policy which would ensure that there was money available in the event of sudden illness, accident or death. This is not unusual. Insurance and life assurance companies are always trying to sell us such things. What struck me was the inappropriateness of such a letter coming from an ecclesiastical insurance company. I thought that a company that existed to serve the Church might have greater confidence in divine providence. I did not expect such confidence – and did not get it – from the financial adviser of another company, who explored with my wife and me the consequences if either of us were to die suddenly, leaving the other partner with two young children. He did cause me to look carefully at the Church's provision for widows but in the end I was unable to accept his life assurance proposals, not primarily because of what they cost, but because ringing one's life around with a wall of policies seemed quite simply to fly in the face of the gospel.

I do not mean that we should not be prudent, but there is a point at which our attitude to the future can become faithless. It was with these thoughts in mind that I came upon a passage from Bishop Horne entitled 'On the blessings of a cheerful heart'. George Horne was born in 1730 and died in 1792. President of Magdalen College, Oxford, at 38, he became vice-chancellor of the university in 1776, Dean of Canterbury in 1781, and Bishop of Norwich in 1790. He was a great preacher whose sermons were often reprinted and his most important work was on a commentary on the Psalms.

In this little piece Horne points to the passages in Proverbs that urge us to be merry. 'A merry heart doeth good like a medicine' he quotes from Proverbs 17.22, which is perhaps the origin of the *Readers' Digest*'s 'Laughter – the best medicine'. And he illustrates the opposite as well: 'Anxiety weighs down the human heart, but a good word cheers it up' (Proverbs 12.25). 'A merry heart maketh a cheerful countenance; but by sorrow of heart the spirit is broken.' And in the apocryphal Ecclesiasticus we find another lovely passage urging us to be merry:

> Give not over thy mind to heaviness, and afflict not thyself in thine own counsel. The gladness of the heart is the life of man, and the joyfulness of a man prolongeth his days. Love thine own soul and comfort thine own heart, remove sorrow far from thee; for sorrow hath killed many, and there is no profit therein. Envy and wrath shorten the life, and carefulness bringeth age before the time. (Ecclesiasticus/ Sirach 30.21–5)

Horne recommends cheerfulness to us as a habit. He stresses habit because he wants us to have more than occasional flashes of merriment that are often succeeded by depression. He recommends the habit of being pleased ourselves and pleasing others, in opposition to a gloomy, discontented cast of mind. He argues for this on two grounds: human and Christian. His first argument is drawn from the body, acknowledging the influence the mind has upon the body and saying that nothing is more prejudicial to the health of the body than grief, when long indulged, and settled into a habit, whatever may have been its cause, great or little, real or imaginary.

He takes another argument from the world and in particular from the beauty of creation. He points to the way in which the blossoms of spring, the glories of summer and the riches with which autumn overspreads the face of a country contribute as much to the satisfaction of the beholder as they do to the farmer's advantage. 'The same genial power,' he says, 'which brings food out of the earth for the nourishment of the animals that walk upon it, arrays it in a colour the most agreeable and refreshing to the eye of man.' And as he beholds the brightness of the sun, the clearness of the sky, the verdure of earth, well-watered pastures clothed with flocks, valleys covered with corn, and woods resounding with the music of birds — as he beholds all this, he asks how anyone can hold that the heart of man should be involved in gloom and melancholy.

In his Christian arguments Horne says that a cheerful disposition of mind is a duty we owe our Maker. It is God's intention that as we contemplate the beauties and glories of the creation, we might be led to make suitable return of gratitude to him. To receive these gifts with a sour aspect and in sullen silence — like some recalcitrant child — is really to throw them back at the bountiful Donor. Bishop Horne is saying that it is not enough to stand and profess our faith in God; we have to demonstrate as well, in our daily living, that we really do trust him, and that the best way to do that is by a merry heart, by the cheerfulness and return of thanks to God for all he has given us. Be glad, Jerusalem: gather together all you that love her: rejoice and be glad you who were in sadness.

FOURTH SUNDAY OF LENT:
For God so loved the world

The adventure of Christian faith begins with our 'yes' to God's invitation. The voice of the shepherd calls us who are the sheep of his own flock. He calls us by name and, when we hear his call addressed to us with such tender love, we respond. First of all there has to be a willingness to hear. Then, when we hear, we must be willing to respond, willing to give our 'yes' to God, no matter how tentative that 'yes' may be. In this way we enter into faith; we believe and we trust, and as we trust so we learn to trust more. We trust and we love, and as we love, and know ourselves as loved, so we love more. And because we love we want to know, to know more of the one who loves and the one whom we love. Faith and love and knowledge – faith in God, love of Christ, the knowledge and wisdom of the Holy Spirit – define the life of a Christian.

From our first hesitant 'yes' to God in Christ we are drawn into his life – we are made like Christ in baptism and we are to be and to become Christ-like in all that we do and think and say, in all that we are. Our lives are to be conformed to Christ and, if we are to be his disciples and come to share his victory, they must be conformed to him. If it is baptism that first makes us one with Christ in his death and in his resurrection, then it is the Holy Communion, the sharing in his Body and Blood, that enables us to grow in conformity with him. This conformity is not an end in itself. There is a purpose in discipleship and a mission for disciples. In personal terms, we are so to live in this passing world that we do not lose the life eternal. Our personal salvation is important. We should not forget that. God so loved that he gave his only Son that whomsoever believeth in him should not perish but have everlasting life. We are the 'whomsoever'.

In traditional terms we could contrast the expectation of the blessed – heaven, paradise, eternal bliss, the vision of God – with the expectation of the damned – hell, the inferno, eternal punishment, exclusion from bliss. We are not, however, to want God because of fear of hell, nor to turn from sin because of fear of punishment, but to love God because he first loved us and to embrace what is right and good because it is right and good. And all this is not an added extra for it is in God that we live and move and have our being, and we are to love God with all our heart and soul and mind and strength. In other words, anything else we do, whatever else we do, comes after, from and because of our love for God. And the mission that is laid upon the disciples is that of bringing everyone into this sort of relationship to God, to the God who definitively reveals his nature and his will in Jesus Christ.

MONDAY OF THE FOURTH WEEK:
Be conformed to Christ

This, then, is our mission and it is one that we should embrace with enthusiasm and with joy. If we love God, we must also love our neighbour, our brother, sister, child, friend, and our enemy, and the casual acquaintance and the stranger. We must love them as Christ loves us, want what is good for them, and want above all else that they should know God, be reconciled to God, and share in the promises of Christ. We cannot be indifferent to the salvation of others. To be indifferent would be disloyal to the faith we profess and the Lord we serve. It is that Lord who will come again to judge the living and the dead. We cannot excise that from Scriptures or the creeds. We cannot rewrite the documents of the Christian inheritance to suit ourselves. All will stand under judgement, but in the last great day Christ will again call his own by name.

We are called to Christian discipleship. The joys of being a Christian are very great, greater than we often imagine, and praise and thanksgiving should be a characteristic of both life and worship. Yet these are also difficult days, a wintry season for faith, and especially for faith that refuses to surrender to fundamentalism and give up the exercise of reason and intellect. The way of the disciple is not easy, and I wonder if we would really have taken up the call if we thought it was going to be easy. Jesus never said, 'Follow me and it will all be plain sailing.' He never said, 'My disciples will be rich and powerful, healthy and free from all pain and suffering.' Quite the contrary. The basis of discipleship is to be like Christ, to be conformed to Christ. Certainly Christ went up to joy and entered into glory but he 'went not up to joy but first he suffered pain and entered not into glory before he was crucified'.

The way of the disciple may well include difficulties of many sorts, doubts, troubles and sufferings. We reaffirm that we have turned to Christ, repented of sin, and renounced evil, but the reality is that we fall into the sin of which we have repented. Sometimes we fall because we are negligent, not taking enough care, failing to think through the consequences of our thoughts, words and deeds. Sometimes we fall into sin because of weakness, especially weakness of will, and sometimes, though we may hope not often, our sin is conscious and wilful, the product of our own deliberate fault. When we fall into sin, we are to repent, to confess, to make amends, to humble ourselves and to seek both forgiveness and reconciliation. This is not easy but it is necessary.

And then there is doubt. We doubt the love and mercy of God, doubt his power, doubt the teachings of the Church, the statements of creed and catechism. Doubt often springs from personal experience, from what we feel – I experience distress, disease, disaster, I feel unloved, uncared for, I feel only the absence of God. The wisdom and experience of the Church, the accumulated wisdom and experience of saints and sinners, tells us that these feelings and experiences are neither new nor exceptional. Doubt is a necessary part of faith, but there can also be a deliberateness about doubt, as if we must seek the Lord when he wills not to be found and to call upon him when he has not drawn near so as to demonstrate the rightness of our unbelief. Discipleship may prove to be complex and occasionally confusing, very rich though and very varied, though for some blessed souls faith is simple. Not for many, however.

TUESDAY OF THE FOURTH WEEK:
Are you able to drink the cup that I am to drink?

God heard the cry of his people Israel in bondage in Egypt and responded with might. He answered the fervent prayer of his people. Day by day, week by week, we pray with confidence to the Father, and at the centre of the prayer is the petition, 'Thy will be done.' This is a prayer for the coming of the kingdom of God. It looks forward to the fulfilment of all that is promised, when the will of God prevails on earth as it does in heaven. Yet it is not an idle prayer, a meaningless utterance. It is — if we pray it with fervour — a genuine, heart-felt request that I may do the will of God, that his will may be all my desire. As the Psalmist says, 'Lo, I have come to do thy will, O God' (Psalm 40.7–8). But what is the will of God for us, and how shall we know it at any particular time?

I once had an essay set for me by a philosopher. This was its title: 'If a man has done what he thinks is his duty, has he done his duty?' Now we might transpose that into the present context and ask, If I have done what I *think* is the will of God, have I actually done the will of God? The answer to both questions involves a further enquiry. What efforts have to be applied to finding out what my duty is or what the will of God is for me? It is very easy to decide what I think God wants me to do and then for me to do it, claiming that it is in fact his will. And some people have gone forward with good intentions, setting out to do what they thought was God's will, and they were wrong. They had mis-understood. And sometimes that misunderstanding came from failure to apply all the effort necessary to perceiving what is truly God's will.

The disciples did this constantly. Indeed, they did it with such monotonous regularity that we must wonder if they ever really listened to what Jesus said. They wanted to call down fire from heaven upon the Samaritan village that would not receive Jesus as he made his way to Jerusalem. They wanted to sit on thrones in judgement. They wanted to protect Jesus from the street urchins, from the cries of the blind beggar, from the clamour of the crowd. Their response to the soldiers who came to arrest Jesus was the drawn sword, and in each of these instances, and many more besides, they got it wrong.

Gradually, they got it right, and beginning from the events reported in the Acts of the Apostles, a body of wisdom has grown up. It suggests that while we may sometimes perceive the will of God for us as we stand alone before him, we will, more often, find it in community, we will find it in common prayer, in corporate waiting on the Spirit of God, in listening, and in dialogue. We will find it by reading Scripture within the community of faith. And the community to which we belong is not just the local congregation, the prayer group, or the parish, but a community of faith that spans both time and space.

There is a test that can be applied to much that touches upon our life as Christians. We need to ask how far what we plan for ourselves enables us to respond wholeheartedly to Jesus' invitation, 'Follow me.' When James and John looked for the principal places in the kingdom, Jesus asked them, 'Are you able to drink the cup that I am to drink?' Jesus himself would willingly have turned away from that cup. In his agony in the Garden he asked that the cup might pass from him. Drinking of it, draining it to the dregs, meant accepting the false accusations of the Jewish leaders, the mockery of the soldiers, the arrogance of Pilate; it meant the lash, the crown of thorns and the cross. The disciple, the one who replies to the question, 'Are you able?' with the words 'I am able', is invited to take up the cross. But when he or she does so it is not to carry it alone. When the weight is great, other hands help, other hands take the load, hands that bear the mark of nails.

WEDNESDAY OF THE FOURTH WEEK:
I will mock at the world

When we approach Christian discipleship with seriousness, we may find that the Lord shakes us. Let me explain what I mean with this story of a thirteenth-century Dominican friar and preacher, Peter Gonzalez. Peter was made a canon of Astorga Cathedral by his uncle, the bishop, at a very early age, a ridiculously early age. He was a very talented young man, but he became a cleric not because he was convinced that he was called by God nor because he wanted to serve God, but because his canonry brought him wealth and power.

The story is told that, as he rode in state, attired resplendently in his robes, to take possession of his canonry, his horse fell. And he fell too, into the mud. The crowd that had gathered to see him pass by now laughed and jeered. Peter was mortified and humbled. He got up from the mud as a changed man. He said, 'Since the world mocks at me, I will mock at the world.' So he gave up his canonry, with its assured wealth and comfort, and became a begging friar and a wandering preacher. The Lord shook him, shook him in love, and turned him to his service. And the words that he now spoke were spoken for God and in the service of God. Peter was a diligent worker. He preached. He saved the lives of prisoners captured in war and the women taken in a siege. He ministered to ignorant peasants and to coarse sailors, and he witnessed to them the love of God that he had himself so vividly experienced.

Our God is not vindictive, not an arbitrary tyrant demanding that his will be done. He is the fountain and source of love, of a love that knows the necessity of discipline and of sacrifice. From the nature of that love, revealed in Christ, and witnessed to by the saints, we can determine whether that which we perceive as God's will is actually his will. The chances are that if his will as we perceive it involves neither service nor sacrifice then we are mistaken and must ask again concerning it. The chances are that if the will of God as we perceive it leads to status, honour, power, wealth and possessions, then we are actually not following his will but our own. And if we perceive it as involving poverty, self-discipline, gentleness, compassion, loving rather than being loved, comforting rather than being comforted, seeking to understand rather than to be understood – then the chances are that we are on the right track, we are following the will of God.

THURSDAY OF THE FOURTH WEEK:
Will only a few be saved?

Asking questions has always been an important way of arriving at the truth. According to the Greek philosopher Plato, Socrates' method of doing philosophy was to ask questions and when he heard the answers to ask more questions, constantly pushing his interlocutors to define the words they were using and so to refine and clarify their thinking. Question and answer was a recognized method of Jewish rabbinic thought.

Consider how often Jesus was asked questions by the Pharisees. At the beginning they were not questions designed to trap him. He was a new teacher. They did not know to which school of thought he belonged. The way to find out was to question him. Remember the questions put to him; they often began by quoting Moses or the fathers, giving some difficult law or hard saying, and asking for his clarification. And it seems that they liked his replies for they asked him harder questions until they began to see that he mocked them, answering a question with a question. I was taught to do that when twenty years ago I was trained in psychotherapy, to answer a question about myself with a question about my patient, and I remember a joke told by psychoanalysts about themselves: 'We are all failed rabbis!'

The purpose of turning the question back upon the questioner was to discover the intention behind the question. It was rarely straightforward. And the questions put to Jesus – like 'Rabbi, is it lawful to pay taxes to Caesar?' – were also not straightforward. First, they revealed the questioners' fear about a challenge to their religious authority, and later an unwillingness to accept the evidence that Jesus was the promised Messiah.

The question remained central in the development of medieval theology and philosophy. The brilliant twelfth-century thinker Peter Abelard explained that by doubting we come to questioning and by questioning we perceive the truth. He thought that there was nothing, no word of Scripture, no teaching of the Church, that could not be legitimately questioned. His view did not prevail – and some of his questions and the answers he gave got him into trouble. Yet questions remained central to the life of the medieval university. Apart from the question-and-answer method employed in lecturing and in writing, there was a marvellous public disputation twice each year and the master undertook to deal with any questions raised by anyone. They could range from really complex and esoteric questions about theology to the smallest details of daily life.

There is a question put to Jesus which, as we look out at our diverse, multicultural, multi-religious modern world, we might also want to make our own: 'Lord, will only a few be saved?' (Luke 13.23). Perhaps we should turn it round and put it to the questioner. 'Do you hope that only a few will be saved?' Or, 'Do you fear that only a few will be saved?' Are you expecting the answer 'yes' or the answer 'no'? It sounds to me as if the questioner – who interrogated Jesus as he made his way from one town to another, heading always for Jerusalem where he would meet his death – was anxious and expected the answer 'yes'. That is the answer he got!

FRIDAY OF THE FOURTH WEEK:
That the world might be saved

Let us stay with Jesus' answer to yesterday's question. What would it mean for us? No matter how confident in our faith we may be, we cannot feel comfortable about the number of the saved being few.

First of all, it is not the will of God that it should be so. Rather than being an overused verse learned in Sunday school and displayed naively on posters and hoardings, John 3.16 is the key to understanding this: 'For God so loved the world that he gave his only Son, so that everyone who believes in him may not perish but may have eternal life.' And verse 17 continues: 'Indeed, God did not send his Son into the world to condemn the world, but in order that the world might be saved through him.'

Second, if we feel at all weak in our faith we might wonder if we will be numbered among the few. Let me offer some consolation here. The Church is keen to offer the assurance of faith. It is important that it should. There is nothing risky about salvation as long as we are maintained in faith within the community of believers. It was a point stressed at the Reformation. In its fear of death, the medieval Church put doubt in people's minds about this; could they indeed be sure of salvation without provision of masses for years after death and without calling on the protective intercession of the saints? The Reformers were unequivocal in their reply. At the same time it is true to say that salvation can be lost, but it can only be lost by deliberate renunciation of faith. We are reminded of this – and reminded of our unworthiness – to ensure that we are not complacent, that we do not claim salvation as a right, but that it is freely bestowed upon us by

God, not because of any righteousness of our own. Yet any sin – let me stress this – any sin and every sin can be forgiven. God has given power and authority to his ministers to declare and pronounce to his people, being penitent, the absolution and remission of their sins. There are no exceptions, no exclusions. We pray that we may be maintained in faith, but if we fall from it, repentance and with it forgiveness is always possible.

Third and finally, if only a few will be saved we must honestly reckon that many we love and care for who do not share our faith will not be saved. This is a hard one, isn't it? I do not think that we have the biblical evidence to support a version of universalism in which everyone will ultimately be saved, by one method or another. In consequence, we must not let up on mission and evangelism. We do need to bring people to the point at which they are able to respond positively to the divine initiative and to find salvation in Christ. I am clear that there will be more people in the kingdom of God than just the card-carrying members of the Church. This is not least because of the ways in which the Church has itself sometimes obscured or deformed the gospel, because of the ways in which we have alienated people by our wranglings and disagreements, because of our inability to communicate the good news of Jesus Christ in a way that is both attractive and persuasive. But though I am clear about this, it must not make us complacent. We must not think that God will sort it all out and we need do nothing. 'Strive to enter through the narrow door,' says Jesus, and that way is the way of Christian discipleship, the way of the cross.

If you feel inclined like the person who questioned Jesus to ask this same question, then ask also why you want to know and consider how Jesus' answer changes how you live, what you believe, and how you will witness to the good news of salvation.

SATURDAY OF THE FOURTH WEEK:
Sheep and goats

The cathedral city of Autun in Burgundy, of which Talleyrand was once bishop, is twinned, rather oddly, with Stevenage. Quite unlike the Hertfordshire new town, it was founded by and derives its name from the Emperor Augustus. From 1120 the bishop began the construction of a church intended to house the relics of Lazarus, brother of Mary and Martha of Bethany, over whom Jesus wept and whom he raised from the tomb. It was not complete when, in 1130, Pope Innocent II consecrated it, and it would not be finished for another sixteen years. The next thing that was added to it was the tympanum over the west door, a masterpiece of Romanesque sculpture, finished in 1135 and graphically depicting the last judgement.

At its centre, dominating the whole scene, is Christ in Majesty. As in so many medieval depictions, Christ glorified is a serene figure, no longer subject to time, as during his earthly sojourn, but set into the context of eternity. With outspread hands the Lord encompasses the scene of judgement taking place beneath his feet. Four angels blowing trumpets summon the dead from their graves. A further angel separates the elect from the damned. The Archangel Michael confronts Satan, who even at this last moment is trying to upset the weighing of souls by pressing on the beam of the scales. Behind Satan yawns the mouth of hell, but it is a small thing, pushed to the viewer's right – Christ's left, of course – a small thing compared to heaven, to the holy city, and to the souls, including Elijah and Mary, in paradise.

The sculpture does not just set out the scene; it provides some interpretation of it. The glorified Lord, the heavenly host and the saints have a rather insubstantial appearance which stresses their spiritual nature and conveys a sense of heavenly harmony. The dead are all naked. The elect, far more numerous than the damned, progress in a peaceful and orderly file. Their faces are turned towards Christ. By contrast, the fear and agony of the damned are expressed in the chaotic poses and irregular composition of the figures. And at hell's gate the devils express their cruelty in monstrous faces and in the straining muscles of their misshapen limbs.

Harmony is therefore contrasted with disharmony and order with disorder. The spiritual is contrasted with the material and the elect with the damned. This is an image understood by medieval men and women and largely disregarded by us – the image of judgement as fulfilment, as the fruition of the saving work of Christ, as the point at which injustice is finally and definitively remedied. If we dwell too much on hell and the supposed torment of the damned (offensive as it might be to enlightened souls of the new millennium who may seriously doubt that anything can be worse than the hells of our own making, the concentration and death camps, the gulag, the killing fields, the darkness of depression and despair) we risk missing the point and failing to see that it depicts the victory of the divine order. That is the point of the sculpture. What we see, what really strikes us as we look at the tympanum is Christ. We see Christ with outstretched hands. Then we see heaven, and last of all we see hell.

Jesus' parable of the sheep and goats is one of the inspirations for this and other judgement scenes, but judgement is not something added on in an arbitrary way to what has already happened. Judgement is a component in all our actions and what is really important, what transcends all other moral issues, is compassion, together with justice, love of neighbour and selfless service. In the Gospels these are described in the works of mercy – clothing the naked, feeding the hungry, giving drink to the thirsty, tending the sick, visiting prisoners. These are the things that count and whatever else our medieval forebears got wrong, they got this right. They knew it was important. They knew that an account had to be rendered, an account in which their sins would accuse them and their deeds of charity would defend them. And they knew that because what they did to the least of their brothers and sisters they did to Christ, so they would, by his grace, be received into paradise. They knew that and that recognition coloured all their daily living. Perhaps their vision cannot be ours, but if it really cannot then we must find some other way to make sense of the command to love one another as Christ loved us and the teaching about the judgement. And that sense must inform and shape our daily living.

FIFTH SUNDAY OF LENT:
The parable of the vineyard

As we turn more clearly in this week towards the Passion of Christ, we may experience a slight sense of uncertainty. It reminds me a little of what has been happening in the novel I read recently about the French attempt to build the Panama Canal. There are a number of murders. Henry Adams is the first person on the scene, by chance it seems, by unfortunate accident. There appears to be some sort of conspiracy and it cannot be long before Adams himself is murdered. But no, a warrant is issued for his arrest; he is accused of two murders. In that moment the reader must weigh up the evidence and decide − is Adams the innocent party, framed by the guilty, or is he the guilty party attempting to blame the innocent? And the question also to be found here is 'Can I trust the narrator, or has he deliberately deceived me, the reader?'

In Luke 20.9–19 Jesus told the people another parable of judgement. The scribes and the Pharisees, with whom he had just been arguing over the source of his authority, realized that he had told the parable against them. Luke is sure that was what he was doing; he is also sure that he was right to do it. But before we decide who is in the right, we must weigh the evidence. There was a strand of confidence in the religious faith of Israel. We find it in those psalms in which Israel, the people of God, gives thanks for the protection afforded by the righteous Lord. 'Many a time have they fought against me from my youth up, may Israel now say, but they have not prevailed against me.' It is a strand of confidence, perhaps even of overconfidence, that offers assurance that all will be well, and it is criticized by the prophets. The religious weigh up what they have – the covenant, the ark, the temple, the round of sacrifices – how then can anything be wrong? And the leaders of Israel addressed by Jesus, the rabbi of Nazareth, may well have cause to feel confident. There were religious extremists around but they managed to steer a course between the demands of nationhood and the limitations of occupation. They were not free to do what they wanted, for there was Herod, and there was Pilate, and behind and beyond both there was Rome. They did the best they could, in difficult circumstances.

Now they listen to Jesus as he tells a parable. They are suspicious of him; he may be a religious extremist, one who could upset this careful balance, deflect them from the middle way. They listen carefully, as we do. Like many another parable, this one starts as a reasonable story in the Eastern tradition of storytelling. It might be entitled 'The Merchant and his Vineyard', in the tradition of the *Arabian Nights*. It is very like the song of the vineyard in Isaiah 5.1–7 which concerned a vineyard prepared with care on a very fertile hill, a vineyard which yielded only wild grapes. The prophet asks the men of Jerusalem to judge between him and his vineyard, and promises that he will remove its hedge, break down its walls and leave it a waste, overgrown with briers and thorns. And Isaiah gives us the key to Jesus' parable: for the vineyard of the Lord of hosts is the house of Israel.

A parable that concerns a vineyard told to the people by a rabbi is therefore a parable about Israel. Jesus' story has much in common with the prophet's song, though here the grape harvest is withheld by the tenants so that the owner gets nothing. He tries to ask for it, but his servants are abused. He sends three messengers; each is wounded, insulted and goes back empty-handed. At last he sends his son, vested with his own authority, and he is killed by the tenants in pursuit of the inheritance. And because of this the owner will come and destroy those tenants and the vineyard shall be given to others. 'Heaven forbid!' the hearers cried. Which hearers? The people, or the scribes and chief priests? Who was it that grasped in a moment that this was a parable of judgement? It seems to have been the scribes and the chief priests, for why otherwise would Jesus then have asked one of those complex rabbinic questions about the meaning of a text (in verses 17–18)?

MONDAY OF THE FIFTH WEEK:
Seeds of doubt

We are those who hear the text today, who listen to the parable of the vineyard. It is set for us in the context of the progression of events that lead to the cross. We are not over-hearing Jesus talking to the people. We have in a way chosen to hear this, and we are on Jesus' side. We do not feel in any way threatened by this parable. We do not doubt for a moment our possession of eternal life. We do not find ourselves to be unworthy tenants. Or could it be one of those moments when we have a good bit of sympathy with the scribes and chief priests for whom every day, every action was a compromise, an exercise in the art of the possible, for whom Jesus' lack of compromise was a problem that could only be resolved by his arrest and death?

Hearers of the word, innocent, uninvolved, we can in a moment find ourselves accused. After all, vine and vineyard belong to the Church's symbolic matrix. I am the vine; you are the branches. My father is the vine-dresser. Every fruitful branch is pruned and encouraged. Every unfruitful branch is cut off and thrown into the fire. Could not the Church, the new Israel, be the vineyard, and we the tenants? No. Heaven forbid.

Perhaps this makes us uncomfortable. That may not be a bad thing in the fifth week of Lent. In a few days we will wave our palms as Christ goes into Jerusalem, and we go too. We will stand by – stand by and watch – as Christ goes to the cross, caught up liturgically, sacramentally, dramatically, emotionally and really in his passion. And nothing there at the foot of the cross is simple and straightforward. This, then, is a little rehearsal, a trial run. Planting the seeds of doubt, of self-doubt in our minds. Would we have shouted 'Hosanna' or 'Crucify', or both? There is a degree of uncertainty today, an uncertainty that calls us to check where we stand.

TUESDAY OF THE FIFTH WEEK:
Light and glory

The account of the transfiguration has been used at various different points in the lectionary cycles. The *Tridentine Missal* had it on Lent 2 and so does the modern Roman rite. The Lutherans and, following them, the American Episcopalians, make it the last reading of the Epiphany season, on the Sunday before Ash Wednesday. A new verse was added to Bishop Christopher Wordsworth's hymn, 'Songs of thankfulness and praise':

> Manifest on mountain height,
> Shining in resplendent light,
> Where from thence thou leddest them
> Steadfast to Jerusalem
> Cross and Easter day attest,
> God in Man made manifest.

The Alternative Service Book had it on Lent 4, accepting that it marks a clear transition in the Gospels as Jesus both reveals his glory and starts to speak of his passion. The new three-year lectionary seems to have lost it altogether. It is, however, a vital part of the transition from ashes to glory and needs our consideration.

> And through the living radiance there shone
> The shining Substance, bright, and to such end
> Full in my face, my vision was undone.

With these words Dante described the experience of looking upon that one Sun that outshone myriad lamps, the divine glory. He differentiates *lux* and *lumen*, the source of light and its manifestation, the substance and the radiance. The shining Substance is of such intensity that Dante's vision is undone, blinded, rendered sightless. He can no longer see. As Christmas is about the light, so the transfiguration is about the shining. As Christmas is about the source, so the transfiguration is about the radiance. Dante, at first, is dazzled; later his vision is strengthened and he is enabled to see.

Our physical experience of light can inform our spiritual understanding. We know that light can blind us. I well remember the warnings about eclipses such as the one I watched a year or two ago. One could not look directly at the sun. Not only would its intensity damage the eye, the damage would be permanent. But when clouds covered the sun with a light veil and the eyes were protected it was possible to see the sun, and to see it with a clear portion removed by the presence, between earth and sun, of the moon. The sun, the source of light, had to be withdrawn behind a veil of cloud and we had to use smoked glass and other devices before it was possible to see. Spiritual realities partake of the nature of light. The glory of the Lord shines. Even his messengers, the angels, shine. In some paintings of the nativity, the Christ-child himself is radiant, a source of light. But to see the Lord, to see not just the radiance but the substance, is too much for creatures who cannot, unprotected, gaze on the Creator.

There is more to the nature of light. I do not mean the fascinating scientific aspects but our multiple experiences of it – the light that blinds, the light beaming from afar that guides us home, the light that protects from danger, the light that penetrates and the light that does not, the brilliance of a single candle in a dark building, the warm glow of many candles, the light too weak for us to see. We do not experience light as a single phenomenon. Our understanding is built up of countless different manifestations and experiences, yet light is one.

God is light and the source of all light. In him there is no darkness at all. If the glory of God was unveiled we would, like Moses, be afraid, turning our faces away, or in a stupor, like the disciples on the mount of the transfiguration. That is, however, not what we experience. Our experience is almost the opposite of that: not too much light but too little. Our experience is, generally speaking, neither the blinding light of the Damascus road nor the dark night of the soul, but a grey monotony in which some spark of brilliance would be welcome. Perhaps we find ourselves where Dante began, waking, midway through life's course, 'in a dark wood where the right road was wholly lost and gone'.

We need a light to see where we are going, to enable us to move. Recounting the story of the transfiguration and affirming its truth, Peter says, 'You will do well to be attentive to this as to a lamp shining in a dark place' (2 Peter 1.19). Peter seems to understand that a darkness, an uncertainty, surrounds the Christians to whom he is writing. Dark places can be unnerving and disorienting. The doorway through which we go regularly and without fear in the light can become, in the dark, an object of fear. Imagination out of control presents all the possibilities for accident, all the possible encounters, from vermin to ghosts. Uncertain, we hesitate, draw back, peer in the darkness, hoping for a surer, safer way. Such moments of hesitation come early in the path of discipleship. The believers, Peter knows, need some reaffirmation, some indication of future glory, a light to dispel the darkness, one that holds the darkness back until dawn comes, until the morning star rises. 'Hang on to this,' Peter tells them, and us. The transfiguration, the manifestation of the power and majesty of the Lord Jesus, is a most effective assurance that Jesus is truly the Son of God and that this majesty belongs to him.

Glory is a sign of fulfilment. Only the winner receives the cup and the acclaim of the crowd; only the victor gets the triumph and the laurels. The glory belongs to Christ. The transfiguration is one of a series of showings, of epiphanies. To the Magi, he was a king; in Jordan, the beloved Son; to the crowds, the voice of a new authority; to the sick, a healer; to the disciples, a master, and on the mountain, God's Son, the fulfilment of law and prophecy. And this is the one we are following, the one whose disciples we are. Ahead of us in the darkness, he shines as a lamp, guiding us along the way, leading us to share his glory.

WEDNESDAY OF THE FIFTH WEEK:
O Jerusalem, Jerusalem

If you look into the background of some paintings of our Lord's crucifixion, you will see Jerusalem not as the city of God but as the city opposed to God. You will see, behind the cross, the walls and towers which stand against Christ. Dominating all is the Temple, with its empty sanctuary and its torn veil. This is the desolate city, the great solitude. This is the city that kills the prophets and stones the messengers of God. O Jerusalem, Jerusalem. Embodied in her is both the rejection of God and fulfilment in God; even the Temple stands for both absence and presence, for rejection and acceptance.

Think for a moment of the story of the temptations of Jesus in the wilderness as Luke tells it (Luke 4.1–13). Jesus is in the desert. The Spirit has taken him there. He has begun his ministry, left his home, left the care of his family. He is in the wilderness like his forefathers Abraham, Isaac and Jacob, and like the children of Israel on their way out of Egypt, journeying to the promised land. The desert, the wilderness, is a place of testing and of temptation, as also a place of knowledge.

'Turn the stones into bread,' says a voice, a voice whose mockery and temptation we will hear again outside a city wall. 'Turn the stones into bread; show that you are the Son of God.' Unsuccessful, the father of lies tries again, offering easy authority and glitzy splendour. For the last equally unsuccessful attempt he takes Jesus on his third recorded visit to the Temple. Each time, the Temple of Jerusalem is a place of revelation; first by the voices of Simeon and Anna; second by Jesus' own words: 'Did you not know that I had to be in my

Father's house?' and third, when he stands on the highest point of the building and dismisses the tempter.

And what happens? What is the result of this third temptation? The very words of Luke's Gospel are these: Jesus returned to Galilee in the power of the Spirit. Though Jesus travels much after that, from one town and village to another, he does not return to Jerusalem, not until after the transfiguration, not until he has talked with Moses and Elijah, and then he sets out resolutely for the city. His progress is resolute but slow. All along the way he engages with the people he meets. Teaches them, heals them, tells them that the kingdom of God has come to them. And he begins to speak of what will happen to him, of what Jerusalem will mean.

The question for us today is whether we are ready to go with Jesus. We have been called and chosen but should we stay a little while longer among the towns and villages? Should we listen for a little while longer to the teachings of Jesus, to make sure we have understood them, fully grasped them, made sense of them? Or are we ready to go resolutely to the city? Do we know what it will mean if we do? Do we know that it is the way of the cross?

If we are not ready, then we should hang back. There is nothing wrong with that. Our time will come. Three times Jesus went to Jerusalem before his triumphal entry, before his Passion. Only after the experience of transfiguration was he able to set his face toward the city. Like him, you must know that the time is right. The holy fast of Lent tries and tests us every year, moves us by pious exercises, towards the point where we say – and say undoubtedly in fear and trembling – I will go with you, Lord; I will go with you this year, and every year, onwards to Jerusalem.

I will go with you. Not alone. When we go, we go together.

When we go, we are disciples. When we go, we follow Jesus who leads us. And as we go we will need the helping and supporting hand, not just his, but also those of the other disciples. That is what it means to be Church, to be the community of faith, the company of disciples. There will be times when we want to turn back, times when weariness touches heart and feet, times when the pilgrim way seems hard and unrewarding and unnecessary, times, even, when we must be carried – though never, never against our wills. Come then, if you will. Share the last stage of this Lenten journey – the fast, the penitence, the turning to God in faith. The Lord is ready to go and leads those who will follow steadfastly to Jerusalem.

Jesus went through the towns and villages, teaching as he made his way to Jerusalem. And we are on the journey through Lent, a journey nearing its conclusion. Both journeys lead to the city that kills the prophets. I live in a city which is considered to be one of the safest in the world; I mean the square mile of the City of London. Round it is the metropolis of London (the Metropolitan Police area), which is also a fairly safe place. I have stayed in a number of cities on the eastern side of the United States. In the biblical Jerusalem you seem to have been safe as long as you were not a prophet. In New York there were no such fine distinctions and when I visited Washington, D.C., there had been a spate of drive-by shootings, random and unexplained. I was warned not to go about after dark, not to take the risk. Yet it is true of any great city that you need to learn where you can go and where you can't. We learn to act with caution.

Given that such caution governs our lives, I wonder how we can set out with confidence on the spiritual journey, the way of discipleship, which is so obviously the way of suffering, the way of the cross. We go steadfastly to Jerusalem and the warning notices say, 'Look out! This is dangerous.' And so you might say, how do I know that it won't be dangerous for me? How do I know that I will be among the saved, among those who, in Jesus' own terms, will squeeze in through the narrow door, who will get in before it is shut? You may ask, is it worth the risk? You may also ask if Jesus is a trustworthy guide who will not lead us astray.

There are three reasons why we should trust Jesus in this.

First, what we are. Far into Lent we may already have forgotten, our possession of life may have reasserted itself. Remember that you are dust and to dust you will return. Remember that, one day, inevitably, without any doubt, we will each be commended to Almighty God, and that the bodies that we so cherish will be committed to the ground or to the elements, earth to earth, ashes to ashes, dust to dust. We are old earth, formed of earth, returning to earth. That is what God has ordained. We need to be realistic about that.

The second reason to trust Jesus is what we have become: a new creation. The Church's burial liturgy does not deny our grief when we face death, our own or someone else's. It doesn't deny that death is a time when we need help, when we need prayers, because we are at last going to be seen for what we are. Hope and fear will mix at the last moment. Will we be acknowledged as a sheep of Christ's own fold, lambs from his flock, sinners of his own redeeming? The funeral services do not deny this anxiety but they also talk of sure and certain hope, of entrance into the land of light and joy, of the fellowship of the saints. They do this because we are baptized into Christ, because he has made a baptismal covenant with us, a solemn agreement of which the baptismal washing – together with the signing with the cross, the anointing, the white robe, and the giving of the candle – is the sign and seal. We have new life. We are born again by the Holy Spirit. Baptized into Christ's death and resurrection we can go, led by him, through the grave and gate of death to our joyful resurrection. This, then, is what we have become – citizens of heaven. We are on pilgrimage because we have a right to be in the heavenly city. We belong to the household of God. Remember you are dust, certainly, but remember also that in Christ you are more than dust.

FRIDAY OF THE FIFTH WEEK:
The testimony of Christ and the witness of the saints

The baptismal covenant means that we are become a people who are constant in the apostles' teaching and fellowship, who gather to share in the breaking of bread and in the prayers. We are a people who resist evil, but we are not perfect. If we fall into sin, we repent and return to the Lord. We are a people charged with the proclamation of the Good News, called to make Christ known as Saviour and Lord, sharing with him in his renewal of the world. We are the people who value others, who seek Christ in all persons and serve him there. We love people and value them because God made them and Christ redeemed them. This is what we have become in Christ: God's own people, the new Israel of the Lord.

The third reason why we should trust Christ and go with him to the city of persecution is what we will yet be. Washed in the blood of the lamb, the city that kills the prophets becomes the city of God. We shall see a new heaven and a new earth. We shall see the Holy City, the new Jerusalem, and we will have the right to be there because we are citizens of heaven and we can take up our rightful place. We are not the enemies of the cross of Christ, and we do indeed look for the one who will transfigure our humble bodies, making them like his glorious body.

Old earth, new earth. We move from one to the other. From sorrow and pain to joy. From dust and ashes to glory. I have told you why we should do it. I must tell you that it isn't easy. Christ could not go up to joy until he had first suffered pain. He could not enter into glory until he was crucified. We are walking the way of the cross. There are no other ways that lead with certainty, with absolute certainty, to the narrow door. The testimony of Christ, the witness of his saints, and my own humble testimony, is that the way of the cross is the way of life and peace, and it is the way we must go.

SATURDAY OF THE FIFTH WEEK:
Venturing forth in love

We may need another witness before we make our final decision. One of my favourite paintings is nothing more than a fragment. There are three figures, two partial, one whole. To the left we see a bit of a red robe, a foot, inverted because the figure is genuflecting, and a couple of toes. To the right and behind the main figure is a man whose head has disappeared, whose left hand holds a walking stick and his right hand an arrangement of beads on a tasselled cord, akin to a rosary. We surmise that these figures are a kneeling St John the Evangelist and a standing St Joseph, whose head seems to have found its way to Lisbon, and we further surmise that this is a fragment of rather a large altarpiece by Rogier van der Weyden of the Virgin and child with saints, painted in the mid-fifteenth century. As it now is it takes its name from another figure, a figure of great beauty and sublime tranquillity. The painting, in London's National Gallery, is called 'The Magdalen Reading'.

Mary of Magdala may be recognized by her attributes, by those signs which point out the identity of this or that saint in a painting. She is richly dressed. Her fur-edged green gown is drawn up to reveal the gold brocade beneath. Beside her, starkly white, is the jar of ointment of the anointing at Simon's house. Her eyes are on her book, itself the expensive product of the scriptorium and the illumination workshop, and it is finely bound. She holds the book through a cloth so as not to damage its binding. Her air of calm, her single-minded concentration on the text, echoes the ability of Mary of Bethany, sister of that busy housekeeper Martha, to sit in rapt silence at Jesus' feet.

This Mary, the Mary of patristic preaching, of the *Golden Legend*, of medieval and renaissance art, is a composite figure. She is the woman who anointed Jesus, a woman of ill repute. She is the sister of Martha, and of Lazarus, raised from the tomb by Jesus. She is the one from whom seven demons were cast out and the one to whom Jesus first appeared as he rose from the tomb. Our forebears were, it seems, uncomfortable with fragments. The unnamed woman needed a name. She needed a history, a family, an explanation of how Simon the Pharisee knew that she was a sinner and of why Jesus so readily forgave her.

Jacobus da Voragine, compiler of the *Golden Legend*, tells us that she was very rich and teaches us that sensuous pleasure keeps company with great wealth. She was, he says, renowned for her beauty and for her riches, and no less was she known for the way she gave her body to pleasure. The identification is not assured but let us stay with it for a moment, for there are few more touching stories in Scripture than this of the penitent sinner who washes Jesus' feet with her tears, wipes them with her hair, kisses his feet and anoints them. Jesus uses this extraordinary incident as an occasion to teach about forgiveness and to reinforce his earlier observation that it is the sick who need a physician, not the healthy.

Jesus contrasts the woman with Simon the Pharisee, the teacher and interpreter of the Law, a member of the religious party that spent so much time watching Jesus and hoping to catch him out. 'You didn't wash my feet,' chides Jesus, 'but she has, with tears for water and hair for a towel. You did not greet me with a kiss, but she has hardly ceased from kissing my feet. You did not anoint my head with oil of gladness but she has anointed my feet.' And Jesus reaches out to Simon, to touch him, to open his eyes and to unlock his heart. 'Do not

see a sinner, Simon, to be shunned, to be turned out, someone whose very touch is contaminating. See someone who
has loved much, too much, too well, whose love has led her
to sin, and to many sins. See a person, Simon, not a case, not
a problem. A person whose very appearance speaks of love.
And Simon, Simon, in your narrow law-abiding self-righteousness, recognize that you risk feeling little love, loving little,
having little to forgive because you have only partly lived.
Live, Simon. Take the risk involved in living and loving.'

I have joined willingly in the medieval process of embroi-
dery, of filling out the dialogue, and I shall soon want to
know about Simon's background and to know what he did
afterwards. Was Simon the Pharisee among those who brought
Jesus to his death or was he, like Nicodemus, a secret disciple?
We don't know. Indeed, we really don't know much of Mary
of Magdala and her composite parts, but I like the reading
Magdalen and she expresses for me the emphatic words of St
Ambrose of Milan:

> She it was, I say, who washed the Lord's feet with her tears,
> dried them with her hair and anointed them with ointment,
> who in the time of grace did solemn penance, who chose
> the best part, who sat at the Lord's feet and listened to his
> word, who anointed his head, who stood beside the cross
> at his passion, who prepared the sweet spices with which
> to anoint his body, who, when the disciples left the tomb,
> did not go away, to whom the risen Christ first appeared,
> making her an apostle to the apostles.

This Mary knew how to love, loved Christ well and gave us
an example that we should follow, that of taking the risk and
venturing forth in trusting love.

PALM SUNDAY

The Palm Sunday liturgy combines two elements that are held in conflict – the triumphal entry into Jerusalem and the passion of the Lord. Liturgy rarely re-enacts events from the life of Christ. It is not a play and it eschews the realism introduced into the mystery plays. It is a sacramental perfor-mance: an outward and visible sign of something essentially inward and invisible. Nevertheless, there are times when a strong element of drama comes into the liturgy. Palm Sunday is one of these occasions.

In its medieval form the blessing of the palms took place ideally in another church. The ceremony of blessing was quite complex with a number of readings, culminating in St Matthew's account of the entry into Jerusalem and a sequence of six prayers for the blessing of the branches of olive, palm and other trees which were to be used in the procession. A whole complex of biblical symbolism was picked up in these prayers. They referred to the olive branch brought back to Noah's ark by the dove, to the palm as a symbol of victory over death, to the olive as the tree that bears the fruit which produces the oil of anointing and as a symbol of peace, as well as to the gospel story of the people meeting Christ and waving branches. The branches were sprinkled with blessed water and censed. Then they were distributed as the choir sang the antiphon *Pueri Hebraeorum* – the children of the Hebrews bearing olive branches went forth to meet the Lord, crying out and saying, 'Hosanna in high heaven.'

The procession then set out and a series of antiphons were sung. The door of the church to which they were going would have been shut. Cantors, often children, on the other side of the door, or sometimes in a gallery, began the hymn of Theodulph of Orléans that I mentioned at the outset (page 1). The cantors sang the verses and outside the church the celebrant and others sang the refrain after the verse. At the end, the subdeacon knocked at the door with the shaft of the processional cross and, as it was opened, the procession entered singing an antiphon that again evoked the children going out to meet the Lord.

After this the Mass began. It is like other celebrations of the Eucharist in Lent except in one respect – the Gospel is the Passion of the Lord as recorded by St Matthew. It was intended to be sung by three deacons: one as narrator, one as the voice of Christ, and one singing the rest, with the choir singing the words of the crowd. This method of singing – the Victoria settings have become standard – together with the act of kneeling when Christ gives up his spirit makes the Passion a little drama, an evocative re-presentation. It is repeated in a similar way on Good Friday.

The Palm Procession and the Passion make for a long service, of course, but it enables us to enter more fully into Jesus' own experience and to recognize how easily the cries of 'Hosanna' turned to those of 'Crucify'. We can enjoy this – if 'enjoy' is quite the right word – and we can understand it; we may be moved by it, and it surely ought to engage our emotions. But in what way can we pray it or use it in prayer? We may do it by a method of prayer called meditation with the application of the senses. It was developed by St Ignatius Loyola who recommended meditations on the mysteries of our Lord's life. So let us examine his approach to the crucifixion.

Some will be able to use this method unaided; others will find that a picture or a cross or crucifix will help. After a preparatory prayer we use our imaginations to see the cross, to see Jesus crucified – loving me – dying for me. It is not just about imagining what it was like but seeing it as the act of salvation, being aware of Jesus' love for us, for his mother, for John, and so on. So we might imagine the wounds in his hands, feet and side; his sacred heart full of divine love. We can go further and see in an imaginative way his love, his patience, his tenderness, and so on. We can see Mary and St John at the foot of the cross. We can imagine the cross as the tree of life with fruits that we can gather.

Our meditation should take us deeper. It is not just about seeing. We should hear as well – the words from the cross, the prayerful silence of Jesus, and the loud cry with which he commends himself to his Father and gives up the spirit. Perhaps we can taste the tears of the onlookers and Jesus' own tears of love. Perhaps we can touch the wood of the cross and feel how Jesus felt and how Mary felt. This Ignatian method ends with a colloquy – a conversation with Jesus, an address to him from the depths of our hearts. You might remember how Don Camillo used to talk to the crucifix above the high altar of his church; well, sometimes, that was a colloquy. This method of prayer, called meditation, engaging our minds and our senses, can easily draw on the experience of the liturgy, for that too involves our minds and our senses.

MONDAY OF HOLY WEEK:
The nearness of saving death

'Do this in remembrance of me,' says Jesus at his last supper with his disciples as he takes bread, blesses, breaks it and shares it. The Apostle Paul tells us that, in doing so, we proclaim the death of the Lord until he comes. During this week we will come to the night in which he was betrayed and on which he instituted the Holy Communion of his Body and Blood. We will feel very close to him at that time and as we share his agony in the garden. The eucharistic mystery is the mystery of the nearness of our Saviour Jesus Christ – the nearness of his death recalled and set forth in the breaking of bread, the nearness of his life-giving sacrifice. The bread of the Eucharist, sometimes called the host, the sacrificial victim, is the sign of Christ's death. Broken and eaten, it is his broken body given for us. Its sacramental complement is the wine, his blood poured out for us.

We have become confused about death recently. Anxious to spare people's feelings, aware of the pain of grief, we minimize the significance of death. We eschew the traditional ceremonies associated with funerals and introduce a self-conscious joy where there should be deep mourning. We do a serious disservice to those about to die or those who are bereaved when, with the best of intentions, we speak of death as nothing at all. Even a timely and well-prepared dying is not a light matter. There are many of life's experiences which are both frightening and exhilarating. Dying cannot be less than living. Every death, like every birth, is of the utmost importance. It is not like going to sleep, moving into another room, or changing trains at Reading Station. Not even Jesus – especially not Jesus – emerges from death unchanged. As his hands and feet continue to be marked by the manner of his death, so his soul, his inner being is marked. The taking of the bread and wine proclaim that death until he comes. So we who participate in the Eucharist day by day or week by week cannot escape being marked by it and Holy Week cannot stop being eucharistic.

But the Eucharist is not only about death. The food is the food of life, the bread of heaven. We eat the body of Christ and receive the blessings of his grace that we may achieve that eternal life which is our inheritance. The cross is the source of that life. Is the life that we call 'eternal' already ours or is it something that is to come? I suspect that we are not presently able to answer that question. Perhaps the question does not have an answer because it is not a real question. It is an enquiry that emerges from our failure to grasp the radical nature of Christianity, the paradox of life-giving death. 'Unless a grain of wheat falls into the earth and dies, it remains alone; but if it dies it bears much fruit' (John 12.24, RSV). 'Take your son, your only son . . . whom you love, and . . . offer him as a burnt offering' (Genesis 22.2, RSV). 'He who loves his life loses it, and he who hates his life in this world will keep it for eternal life' (John 12.25, RSV). 'If we have died with Christ, we believe that we shall also live with him' (Romans 6.8, RSV). 'While we live we are always being given up to death for Jesus' sake' (2 Corinthians 4.11, RSV). 'We know that we have passed out of death into life' (1 John 3.14, RSV). 'I died, and behold I am alive for evermore' (Revelation 1.18, RSV).

When we kneel in adoration at the Eucharist or when the Blessed Sacrament is exposed for veneration, when we adore him who is the firstborn of the dead, then we encounter that paradox. To opt for anything else, anything simpler, anything easier to understand, is to miss the point. The mystery of the nearness of Christ is the Easter mystery of life-giving death.

TUESDAY OF HOLY WEEK:
I saw water flowing

The key to Holy Week, therefore, is the paradox of life-giving death, of understanding at last what we first looked at in the first week of Lent, that the way of the cross is the way of life and peace. The verses from the Gospels, Epistles and the Book of the Revelation quoted yesterday state that paradox. We minimize it when we reduce the difference between life and death and we grasp it most clearly when we are willing companions with Christ in his sufferings. It is Christ's death into which we are baptized, though this is not the only meaning of baptism. The font is a tomb. The water of baptism is the water of death that closes over the Egyptians and which could so easily have brought disaster to Israel. So if this Holy Week is eucharistic, it is also, in all its days as in its culmination at the Easter Vigil, baptismal. The water that brings death if we are submerged in it is the same water that cleanses and revives us, that washes and refreshes us. Just like the Eucharist, baptism is a sacrament that springs from the cross. John tells us that when the side of Jesus was pierced there came forth water and blood.

One liturgical ceremony which uses water but which is largely obsolete is the asperges. It dates from around the ninth century. It involves the sprinkling of holy water – that is water to which a little salt has been added which is blessed by a priest in the name of the Church – on the altar and on the people before the main celebration of the Eucharist on Sunday. The chant that accompanied the rite came from Psalm 51: '*Asperges me*', 'purge me with hyssop, and I shall be clean; wash me, and I shall be whiter than snow.' During

Paschaltide, the Easter season, the chant was '*Vidi aquam*': 'I beheld water issuing out from the temple, on the right-hand side, and all to whom that water came were saved.'

The medieval mind was quick to make connections. The medievals spoke a language in which we are not fluent, the language of symbols which has its own syntax and grammar. Jesus spoke of the destruction of the temple and its rebuilding in three days. Lest we fail to catch his meaning, the gospel writer tells us that he was speaking not of the Temple that Herod built but of his own body. Why? Because there is no need for a temple once God has become incarnate, man for us. The place of God's abode, of God's presence, is the person of Jesus of Nazareth. We need only think of Luke's account of the annunciation. The angel says to Mary that the power of the Most High will overshadow her. That word 'overshadow' is the one that is applied to the Spirit of God brooding over the waters of creation and the Divine Presence within the tent as the children of Israel made their way through the desert. Jesus is the temple. Ezekiel sees the water of life flowing from the temple. The side of Jesus is pierced on the cross – the right side, of course – and from the wound flows water and blood.

Water itself has a rich symbolic value, from the waters of creation onwards. Jesus turns water into wine. He washes his disciples' feet in water just as Pilate washes his hands. It is deep water that the psalmist fears and concerning which he cries out. And in the end of all things John sees the river of the water of life, bright as crystal, flowing from the throne of God and of the Lamb. In its waters grows the tree of life and the leaves of the tree were for the healing of the nations. The Lord of life is given up to death and he who promised living water is given vinegar to drink. The Passion of our Lord, like some mighty torrent, some great flood, sweeps us along and away, drowns us and yet saves us. Where life is lost, there life has been restored.

WEDNESDAY OF HOLY WEEK:
A bride in blood

A lesson sometimes read at weddings comes from the letter to the Ephesians 5.21–33. In it the Apostle Paul likens the relationship of husband and wife to that of Christ and the Church. The thrust of his argument – and the reason why the lesson is not often used – is that wives should be subject to their husbands and, less controversially, that husbands should love their wives. It is not merely by way of illustration that Paul uses the language of body and bride about the Church for he is clear that Christ loves his Church as a bridegroom loves his bride.

This theme of unity and love is already prepared in Scripture. The divine word, the creating power that goes forth from God, loves the humanity it has brought into being. Wisdom celebrates a marriage with humankind. Here, however, the image is reversed: wisdom is the bride, the fairest of women, to be sought and courted, a pearl of great price. And Christians have always found in the Song of Songs, the canticle of the lover and the beloved, an expression and celebration of the love between Christ and his Church.

The divine lover is Christ and the beloved of his choice is the Church. John the Baptist calls himself the bridegroom's friend, the best man. He stands at the bridegroom's side, he hears his voice and rejoices to hear it. Like many a best man, he undertakes preparations for the wedding, and does so with joy. When the day of the wedding comes, it is the bride and groom who stand in the light, and not the best man. Jesus uses very similar language. So long as he, the bridegroom, is with them, the disciples have no need to fast and mourn, but

rejoice at the glad tidings. One day, Jesus warns, the bridegroom will be taken away. Then will come the time for fasting
and sorrow. Then the bride is left alone with her burning
longing for the beloved, and her loneliness may last for a long
time, for no one can tell when the bridegroom returns. The
great banquet, the wedding feast, the marriage feast of the
Lamb, of which the Scriptures so often speak, belongs not to
the mean time but to the end time, not to now but to then.

This image of the Church as the bride of Christ is not
simply a way of speaking, a metaphorical or analogical way of
expressing a deep, complex and little understood relationship.
As we hear it set forth we are intended to find in it the
symbols, shadows and echoes that express and spring from
our own experience of love and of marriage. But there is
more. The Church is a spouse of blood, or rather a spouse
whose marriage, whose mystical union is made in blood. The
cross is the place of consummation of this marriage and its
fulfilment – the marriage of the Lamb – is foretold by John
in the Book of the Revelation. The lover of the Church is
also her redeemer. His wooing cost him his life. She was won,
made his, purchased at a most costly price. She becomes what
she is, the bride destined for the bridegroom, as a result of the
shedding of his blood. This is her baptism, the source of her
life, her love, her fruitfulness.

Much as we would prefer it, we cannot find – even in the
age of AIDS – an image that can be a more antiseptic substi-
tute. The Church is a spouse in blood. In his sermons on the
Song of Songs, the Cistercian monk, John of Ford, gives the
Church these words:

I was redeemed by your blood, washed in your blood,
given your blood to drink, and by it made mystically

drunk. Through it I hold within my heart the surest pledge of eternal restoration. The blood of my spouse is both the price of my redemption and the laver of my purification; it is the cup that sustains my exile and at the same time a strong incentive to my love being such a clear proof of his love.

Christ's blood, then, is the assurance of his love, that intense love that is always at work in the Church transforming, purifying and renewing, for Christ loves the Church as much as he loves his own body which bears the marks of his Passion. But where do we find that intensity of love when the Church, the body of Christ, faces her divine lover? John of Ford again provides the bride's words: 'I whisper into my spouse's ear and his blood adorns my cheek.' A whisper, a kiss, an embrace – the language of a closeness to Christ that should mark every aspect of the Church's life as the blood of the bridegroom adorns the cheek of the bride.

What we do with blood is wash it away. We remove its mark, its stain, its distinctive taste and smell. We wear protective gloves. We bandage the wounds that bleed. Ultimately, we take down the bleeding body, pale through loss of blood, and bury it. And a nightmare, the very stuff of horror stories, is the bloodstain that will not go away, that constantly reappears, soaks through anything intended to cover it and defies even the strongest of cleaning agents.

Such is the blood of Christ shed for his Church, blood which stains the Church, blood which adorns the Church. It refuses to allow us to turn the Church into a club, a gathering of like-minded people, a charitable organisation or an agent for social change or personal growth. The Church is the bride of Christ, a spouse in blood whose union is renewed each time we drink the cup of salvation. We are bound up with Christ – Christ crucified – and that is a reality that touches all that we do and all that we are, and compels us to look forward to the fulfilment of that union, the marriage feast of the Lamb.

MAUNDY THURSDAY – IN THE EVENING:
Sit here while I pray

There is nothing active that we can do on this night of betrayal. Ours is a passive role. We wait and it, the act or rather the series of actions that make up the Passion and death of the Lord, will be done for us, perhaps even in spite of us. 'Sit here while I pray,' says Jesus to his disciples as he goes further apart with Peter, James and John, with his soul sorrowful unto death. 'Allow me to wash your feet,' he tells Peter. 'You need do nothing; I must do it for you. If I do not, you have no part in me.'

'Take this, this is my body. Drink this, this is my blood.' So Christ gives himself with his own hand, and all we need do is extend our open hands to receive what is given. 'Sit here while I pray.' 'Come, we must be going.' There is nothing we can do except, with heavy hearts, witness Christ's suffering and death. With heavy hearts, for though we know the victory will come, though we know the day of resurrection will dawn, though we are not those who live without hope, yet in these days of Holy Week we must enter into the Passion. We must feel and know why Christ died, and feel and know that it was for us and our salvation.

So on this Maundy Thursday allow yourself to be a witness. In imagination and in liturgy witness Christ in the person of his priest as he sets aside his robes to wash feet, girded in a towel. Listen to Peter's protestation: 'Not you, Lord, washing my feet!' Be a witness as Christ in the person of his priest takes bread and wine and shares his broken body and his spilled blood. And pray for those who on this night, by virtue of their office, act in Christ's person, frail vessels without merit but filled with his power, assured – thank God – that the unworthiness of the minister does not effect the validity and fruitfulness of the sacraments.

May we not also see Judas slip away to confirm his compact and to discharge the act of betrayal, and know that we, who have performed similar acts, cannot prevent this one? And even if we plead with Peter that we will never be unfaithful, do we not know that we have been, perhaps now are, certainly will be? Sit awhile and wait as Jesus prays, 'Abba, Father, all things are possible to thee; remove this cup from me; yet not what I will but what thou wilt.' Watch and pray that you will not enter into temptation, and do so knowing, knowing so well, the painful, agonizing truth of what Jesus says: 'The spirit indeed is willing, but the flesh is weak' (Matthew 26.41, RSV). Be a helpless witness to Judas' kiss, strike out in blind ineffectual anger in Jesus' defence, and watch him led away to certain death for us and for our salvation. 'Sit here while I pray; sit here while I go to my trial, my shame, my pain, my death. There is nothing that you can do for me, for what is needful I must do for you.'

GOOD FRIDAY – AT THE
TIME OF THE PASSION

In London's Victoria and Albert Museum, near my favourite artefact – the painted limewood effigy of Jesus riding the ass which must have graced a Palm Sunday procession in sixteenth-century Germany – you will find a reredos, an altarpiece, of the Passion of the Lord. It is today detached from any altar, no priest stands before it to offer the eucharistic sacrifice, no candles flicker before the nearby statues of the saints, no ministers wear the vestments in the glass-fronted cases. This reredos was the product of devotion to the Crucified Redeemer. There at the foot of the cross you can see the portly figure of the donor, with tonsured head and neatly pleated canon's surplice. Above him and on each side of him, the drama of the Passion is played out as five large scenes, and a further ten scenes within them take us from Judas' act of betrayal to Christ's bursting from the tomb.

As you pass through the gallery, you are invited to stop, to look, to see, and as faith informs your looking, befriending your outward sense, so you will find here something more than an object displayed in a museum. You will find an expression of our faith and of the devotion that motivates us. Stay with me awhile on this Good Friday and let the reredos guide your meditation.

To the left, two soldiers whip the Lord. He is tied to a pillar. One soldier roughly pulls his hair. And the whips – they are vicious-looking things – cats of many tails with knots that bite into the flesh. It is too much even to imagine the pain they inflict. But look behind, where Judas gives the traitor's kiss, and where the soldiers mock the blindfolded king and give him a crown of thorns. Look carefully, for it is not often that we contemplate the Passion. The agony of Christ began last night when he already knew what the day would bring, when his sorrow was so great that it was sorrow unto death. He was shaken – deeply, deeply shaken – by anxiety and sadness. Perhaps you have been there. Do we not in a way know what he experienced, and does he not know the anguish, the sadness, the loss of all confidence that sometimes shakes us? And as if this was not enough, the anticipation of suffering, there was Judas. Judas was not an enemy – that would have been easier to bear – but he was, as the psalmist says, mine own familiar friend with whom I broke bread.

The second large scene of the reredos shows Jesus on his way to Calvary, carrying the cross, and roughly handled by two soldiers. He has his own robe again but he wears the prickly crown. The background scenes show the trial, that mockery of justice, that exercise in vengeance. Pity Jesus as he walks to his death knowing – for who in Roman Jerusalem did not know – the horrific nature of death by crucifixion.

The central scene is, of course, the crucifixion itself, and it is amazingly rich in detail. There is a crowd around the foot of the cross. Mary, the mother of Jesus, is comforted by one of the other Marys and by John. The soldiers dice and brawl. Mary of Magdala clings to the foot of the cross. Longinus – that is the name tradition gives to one of the soldiers – thrusts his lance into Christ's side. On each side of the Crucified Redeemer are the thieves. Demas, the good thief, has his eyes turned to Jesus from whom he receives the promise of being in paradise today. The other thief is contorted – his ugly, twisted body reminiscent of those of the damned we have seen disappearing into the gaping mouth of hell in some medieval last judgement. Above the Saviour the letters of the superscription INRI – *Iesus Nazarenus Rex Iudaeorum* – Jesus of Nazareth, the King of the Jews.

In one of the background scenes, we see Joseph of Arimathea, Nicodemus and others, secret followers of the rabbi, taking the body down from the cross – this is known as the deposition – lowering it gently down wrapped in a great winding sheet. This is the moment that gives rise to some of the most touching products of the sculptor's art – the Virgin *pietà*, holding in her arms the body of her dead son, an extraordinary contrast with the Virgin tenderly holding the infant Jesus. The last scene for our meditation today is the entombment. Joseph and Nicodemus lay the body in the tomb. Again there is a crowd, women mostly, disciples as well. One woman holds the crown of thorns removed from Jesus' head and the three nails that penetrated his hands and feet. It is a scene of unmitigated sorrow. Every face reveals deep grief. But above and behind this scene is another one that shows us, in parallel, what is really happening – there is Jesus, banner in hand, standing before the open mouth of hell, and out from that mouth come the naked souls released by Christ from death's bondage.

We need to contemplate this scene, this series of scenes. We may see it there in the museum. We may look at other pictures. We may create it in our imaginations, taking details from the gospel accounts. However we do it, we must be enabled to come to the foot of the cross – as we can in today's liturgy – and to know that it is not a matter for intellectual assent, not a thesis proposed for discussion, not a subject for council or committee, but the central event of our redemption – and there is no way that it can be sanitized. It is an occasion of blood, pain, tears, fear, cowardice, but also of courage, self-sacrifice and faith in God.

THOUGHTS ON THE WOUNDS OF CHRIST

First Reflection

Holy Week tends to see innumerable performances of the Bach *Passions*. A less well–known Passiontide piece is the *Membra Jesu Christi* of the German composer Dietrich Buxtehude. A profound and lively faith was a marked feature of Catholic Christianity in the seventeenth century of Buxtehude's childhood, youth and adulthood. The spiritual tide flowed vigorously though, as the century wore on, it did so with less creativity. It was the time of disciples rather than masters. The influence of Cartesian rationalism created a dis-trust of the mystical and irrational. The tragedy of Jansenism in France had even brought Christian asceticism into disrepute, pushing spirituality towards a deep austerity, to exaggeration and to unnatural severity. One devotion, however, came to fill the gap, to resolve the differences between increasingly rigid religious schools. It began in a way with Augustine of Hippo, who observed that the heart of Jesus, pierced by the lance, shed its blood for the remission of our sins. Bernard of Clairvaux, William of St Thierry and Richard of St Victor, and later Mechtilde, Gertrude, Anthony of Padua, then Tauler and Suso, spoke of the heart of Jesus as a refuge and a shelter offered to the poor hearts of men and women. From these medieval developments there flowed a subterranean stream through almost the whole of Catholic thought during the Counter-Reformation – that stream was devotion to the sacred heart of Christ. It was, we may suppose, an extension of the devotion to the five wounds of Christ; developed by St Bernard's devotion to the humanity of Christ and to his

Passion, it gained significance from the stigmata received by St Francis of Assisi. It takes us to the foot of the cross where hangs not the majestic Christ of earlier and more optimistic ages, but the bloodied, broken body of the Redeemer, with its pallid hue, near death, if not actually dead. Beneath the cross we kneel and hail the dying Lord: '*Salve mundi salutare*'.

See there, his feet. How often we have watched him stride forward and followed behind. These feet have known the dust of village after village. He told us to cast off the dust from our feet if they did not make us welcome coming in his name. We never saw him do that – he who would not let us bring down fire on the Samaritan village which would not admit him. These feet wore sandals that John counted himself unworthy to untie. These feet were washed with tears by the woman at Simon the Pharisee's house, washed with her tears and dried with her hair, and as she wept she kissed them and then anointed them. These are the feet at which we sat, we and so many others, to hear his teaching. We never washed his feet but he washed ours. Now look – look at them. See how the cruel nail goes through them. See how the blood stains the wood of the cross. O sweet Jesu, blessed Lord, do not drive me from your holy feet.

Second Reflection

Another familiar devotion within the Catholic tradition is that called the Stations of the Cross. Fourteen stations take us from the condemnation of Christ before Pilate to his entombment. It perhaps began as pilgrims to Jerusalem followed the Via Dolorosa and, returning home, wished to continue the devotional practice. Each station involved – and still involves – the recitation of prayers and meditation on aspects of the Passion.

It was particularly popularized by the members of the Franciscan order.

Although it is sufficient to erect fourteen numbered crosses around the church or cloister to enable the faithful to follow the path, yet the stations have been embellished by the artistic imagination, ranging from simple, sometimes rather gaudy or sentimental pictures, to marvellous carvings, or even to tableaux, such as those to be found on Italy's holy mountains. Along the way, leaving Pilate's house, Christ carries the cross. He meets his blessed Mother. Simon of Cyrene is pressed to carry the cross. The woman called Veronica wipes his face. He addresses the weeping women of Jerusalem. He is nailed to the cross, hangs crucified on Calvary's hill. He gives up his spirit and his broken body is taken down from the cross and laid in a borrowed grave.

Three times along the way of the cross Jesus falls. He falls through exhaustion. His Passion, his deep suffering began in earnest at the last supper with his disciples. He knew then that this was the time appointed. He struggled with betrayal. This was not the work of an enemy – no, it was his own familiar friend, with whom he broke bread, with whom he shared wine. He struggled with the knowledge of what the next day would bring. That time spent in the garden is called the agony as Jesus was torn between obedience to the Father and escaping from it all. There was, it seems, no agony, no struggle, when the first Adam readily succumbed to temptation. The second Adam struggled and accepted the will of his Father. There is no play–acting here but a surrender to the divine will which was costly. Already weakened by this spiritual and emotional struggle, Jesus is then physically weakened by his treatment at the hands of his accusers and of the brutish soldiers. Jesus falls beneath the weight of the cross. A simple fall on London's pavements, tripping over a curb or caught out by uneven paving, and we have to deal with torn clothes, torn flesh, sprained ankles. But there was no possibility of hailing a cab. Goaded by the soldiers, Jesus had to struggle on with grazed knees, with bleeding knees, with aching limbs, struggle on to Calvary. *Salve Jesu, rex sanctorum*. Hail, promised hope of sinners.

Third Reflection

When St Francis of Assisi received the stigmata – the marks of the Passion upon his body – he hid them. They were not to be seen. Not something to boast of. This was a gift of grace, divine acknowledgement of Francis' great devotion to the Passion of the Lord. They were not just marks or holes. They were wounds and the wounds bled, not always but periodically, especially on Fridays and in Lent and at Passiontide. The wounds did not become septic but they would not respond to any sort of treatment. It was difficult to hide them but somehow Francis succeeded and there were those who doubted that he had received them. About 300 people are reputed to have received the stigmata; about sixty of them are counted among the recognized saints of the Church. Francis was the first for the phenomenon was unknown before the appearance of the great devotion to the Passion of Christ of which we have been speaking.

Salve Jesu, pastor bone. Good shepherd, tending the sheep, laying down your life for the sheep. Good shepherd, calling us by name, knowing us, searching for us when we are lost, gathering us into your fold. What are these wounds, good Jesu? Wounds of love, suffered for us. How can we look at these hands and bear to see them so cruelly torn? How can we look and not remember how they rested on the heads of the children as you blessed them, how you took the blind man's hand in yours, how you extended your hand to raise up the daughter of Jairus and helped the widow's son from his bier? How can we look and not see them as you held the bread, and broke it, and shared it with us? How can we bear to see them now – hands we know so well, carpenter's hands with the calluses of work, gentle hands swift to bless? We would now take them in our hands and kiss them, mingling our tears with your blood. May we see and feel and know these hands when we fall and must be raised up, when we are in danger and need to be defended, when we are lost and need a hand to hold, when we are in pain and need a hand to squeeze, when we face death and need a hand to guide. *Manus sanctae, vos amplector.*

Fourth Reflection

There was a tradition, apparently without foundation, that the eighteenth-century author and hymn-writer Augustus Montague Toplady wrote 'Rock of ages, cleft for me, Let me hide myself in thee' while sheltering from a storm in the Mendips. From my viewpoint, within the catholic tradition of Anglicanism, Toplady is an unattractive character, a follower of John Wesley who then turned on him, bitterly attacked and opposed him when he himself converted to extreme Calvinist views. But his character and beliefs have no effect on my pleasure in his best-known hymn, a hymn that sets out a profound theology of grace. Did Toplady know the *Salve latus salvatoris*? It seems unlikely, but there is clear agreement between the product of catholic devotion to Christ in his Passion and that emerging from the extreme Calvinist insistence on the primacy of grace to which we contribute nothing.

It is addressed to Jesus as the cleft rock of ages – the image of the rock is found in the Psalms and also in the rock from which water gushed in the wilderness of Exodus. It acknowledges the double flow, the water and the blood, which pours from the side of Christ, as that which alone can wash filthy hearts – *corda sordida* – and wash away both the guilt and the power of sin. Toplady's Christian brings nothing to the cross, for he or she has nothing worth bringing. Labour, obedience to the Law, zeal for the gospel, tears of repentance; none of these atone for sin. Christ is the one who saves and Christ alone.

> Nothing in my hand I bring,
> Simply to thy Cross I cling;
> Naked, come to thee for dress;
> Helpless, look to thee for grace;
> Foul, I to the fountain fly;
> Wash me, Saviour, or I die.

At the hour of death – an hour much neglected today when we find it hard to think about dying – the Christian, catholic or Calvinist, asks for protection. *Membra Christi* asks that our breath may enter the side of Christ, like hiding in the cleft of the rock; that there might be found a sure refuge and a place of safety. And that is what Toplady wants: 'Rock of ages, cleft for me, Let me hide myself in thee.'

Fifth Reflection

We have moved away from the heart as the centre, the heart of our being. We think with our brains; or at least we think that is where we think. We feel in our gut; know there the butterflies of nervousness, the twisting pain of anguish, the gut reaction of horror and rejection. The heart is the organ that pumps the blood, circulating it in a way that was unknown until William Harvey discovered it at the famous hospital next door to my church. We may still have a broken heart, true, but the heart is not involved in much else beside affairs of the heart.

But when John Henry Newman said *cor ad cor loquitur*, heart speaks to heart, he meant an intimacy, a knowledge of another person, that was not cerebral or sexual, but was profoundly intimate. More than a meeting of minds; a meeting of individuals in the totality of being, a meeting called love. Love is one of the most problematic of words, for human love is, it seems, so fragile, so easily broken, so swiftly trampled by unthinking feet. Love that carries our hope seems too weak, too insubstantial for the burden. When we love – heart open to heart – we are at our most vulnerable, most easily wounded. It is inevitably those we love who hurt us most easily. Love is the prize to be grasped which eludes us. But against this all too human experience, the 'torment of love unsatisfied, the greater torment of love satisfied', there is another love. Not, in fact, one love among many, but the original form and source of love, love that does not veer wildly from desire to indifference, from solicitude to contempt, a love that is not tormented and unfulfilled – the love of God for us, the love that pours from the wounded heart of Christ.

The Apostle Paul teaches us about it – Paul who knows suffering, knows despair, knows frustration. Paul's striving spirit has seen and knows that his effort is not in vain because of the love of God. He asks, what is certain? What will hold when all else fails? Not knowledge, for we have lost knowledge

in information. Not wisdom, for wisdom has gone the way
of knowledge, a stream of speech without silence, of words
without meaning. Nothing seems lasting, nothing seems
certain, all is fashion, changing, transient, relative. And into
this flux Paul brings a powerful and unexpected note of
certainty, brings something to which we may hold fast. Who,
he asks, who or what, what possible combination of events or
powers, the foreseen or the unforeseen, can separate us from
the love of God? Hail, O heart of the highest king, fount and
source of love. Let that love engulf me, uphold me, sustain
me. Let my heart be moved by your heart. Let it respond in
love to your sweet heart. May it find strength to fix itself on
you, O blessed Jesu.

GOOD FRIDAY – IN THE EVENING:
Into the labyrinth

A maze, like that at Hampton Court, is a source of enormous fun. Round and round we go, ignoring those who tell us to put out a hand to this side or that and only ever to turn to the left or is it to the right. There is always a method that will get us to the middle, apparently, but that really takes away the element of exploration, of trial and error, of meeting the same people over and over searching for the way forward. In our ordered lives, a little innocent disorder does us good. In the hands of a talented director and with deft camerawork, the maze can become nightmarish, as a character is pursued and runs blindly onwards, caught in the dead ends, the culs-de-sac, made irrational by fear. Then the maze ceases to be a source of fun and becomes labyrinthine and the labyrinth really is the stuff of nightmares.

The English word *mase* is of uncertain origin, but it is linked to 'amazed', meaning astonished or bewildered, and it stresses confusion, annoyance, a difficult process. By the time of Chaucer, that is by the fourteenth century, the maze appears to be well known in England but the Cretan labyrinth less so. I say Cretan, for this is the best known of all labyrinths, that of Minos the King of Crete which, designed by Daedalus, imprisoned and concealed the Minotaur, a monster with the body of a man and the head of a bull, product of the union between Minos' wife Pasiphaë and a handsome bull. Minos fed the Minotaur with the young men of Athens. Eventually there came Theseus who, with Ariadne's help, found his way through the hitherto inextricable labyrinth, and caused the Minotaur to choke on a ball of pitch before doing him to death. And it was to escape subsequent imprisonment in the labyrinth that Daedalus and Icarus made the wings that ultimately led to Icarus' death.

This may seem an odd subject for Good Friday – an exercise in Greek mythology rather than Christian theology; but Christianity very early took up the symbol of the labyrinth, creating them from multicoloured stones laid on church floors and sometimes set into the walls. One in North Africa dates from the fourth century. They are found in churches in Italy, France, England and Germany and in many monasteries as well. Some are surrounded with the signs of the zodiac and the symbols of the seasons. One in Pavia includes a depiction of Theseus and the Minotaur. They were often large. Over 12 metres in diameter are the labyrinths inlaid in the floors of Chartres and Amiens cathedrals and the one at Auxerre, now lost, was of similar size. At Piacenza an inscription tells us:

> This labyrinth reveals the structure of the world,
> Free to him who enters
> But very narrow to him who returns.
> He who is ensnared by this world
>   and is weighed down by the delights of vice,
> Will find it hard to solve the riddle of life.

And another inscription takes our understanding a stage further:

> Look upon this mirror and behold in it thine
>   own mortality!
> Thy body shall become dust and food for the worms,
> But thou thyself shalt live eternally; this life is
>   hard to live.

Beg and pray to Christ that thy life may be
    lived in Christ.
That by the Easter festival thou mayest be
    awakened and come out of the labyrinth.
By these five lines of verse I instruct thee in
    the secret of death.

The maze is not just darkness and confusion. No. It simulta-
neously combines artistry and confusion, order and chaos,
inertia and progression. The labyrinth, whether that which
has many paths which create confusion, doubt and frustration
as one ambiguity succeeds another or that which has only
one path leading inexorably, by its very structure but by the
longest possible way to the centre – the labyrinth provides a
picture of life as many, perhaps all, experience it. In its
mythological origin, however, the labyrinth speaks of death.
Within it dwells the Minotaur. Not only must the path be
navigated but one must avoid the necessarily fatal encounter.

Perhaps this is why it appealed to our medieval forebears.
They knew life's uncertainties and often found themselves
perplexed by its twists and turns, downcast as they observed
themselves first close to the goal and then oddly moving away
from it. They knew that death waited for them; they remem-
bered they were dust returning to dust. The anxious father
rushing the newborn to the font, the midwife baptizing in
the home, feared for this life and for the life to come. The
labyrinth set out the secret of death; it also set forth the secret
of life.

As Theseus entered into the Minotaur's lair, so Jesus of
Nazareth did not flee from the encounter with death. Theseus
was compelled to go, one of the Athenian youths offered to
Minos; Jesus chose to go. Until quite late in the gospel story

he could have avoided death, could have satisfied the Jewish leaders of his intentions and reassured Pilate. He chose not to but chose instead to follow his Father's will and so to encounter that force which was unleashed in the creation from the first act of disobedience.

Accounts of our redemption often, and rightly, stress the sacrificial nature of Christ's self-offering; he is both priest and victim. Others point to symmetry between Jesus and Adam, a sort of mirror image. Ambrose said: 'Adam was formed from the virgin earth, Christ was born of a virgin. Adam was made to God's image, Christ is the image of God. Folly came through a woman, through a woman came wisdom. Adam was naked, Christ was naked, Death came by a tree, life by Calvary's tree.' They see Christ's agony in the garden as the moment when he does the very opposite of Adam's easy surrender to temptation. Others again offer more complex theologies of redemption.

The labyrinth idea makes Christ a hero, precursor of the noble knight seeking out the distressed damsel. Christ is held up as one who was courageous; not unafraid but able to go on despite fear; one who did not shrink back. What happens in the labyrinth is hidden, however. And that too accords well with the silence of Scripture about what happened between his death on the cross and the moment of resurrection. Behind the cross is a cosmic struggle between life and death.

The death is real. Christ dies. Christ experiences the moment of uttermost abandonment. Resting always upon God, his strength and his strong tower, Jesus found himself bereft of that support as he took to himself the sins of the world. The All-Holy One cannot admit within the Divine Being that which rejects life. God cannot be party to sin. Jesus utters the familiar words of the psalm: 'My God, my God, why hast thou forsaken me?' Not to invoke for us that psalm's promise of deliverance, twenty-two verses in, but because it expresses so exactly, so forcefully, so immediately all that he is experiencing; 'Why art thou so far from helping me, from the words of my groaning?' The stone closes over the tomb of Christ as he is deep within death's labyrinth. It looks like failure. It looks like defeat. The tears are real; the bitter grief of Mary and of the other women; even angels shed tears in many a depiction of the crucifixion or else veil their faces with their wings, unwilling to look upon the Crucified. Yes, it is a scene of desolation. But unbeknown to us, save by the evidence of the resurrection, Christ struggles with death and overcomes the ancient foe, as Theseus, guided by Ariadne's thread and armed with the ball of pitch, found, did battle with and overcame the Minotaur. Christ's victory does not mean that all mystery is removed from life and from death. What is removed is the terror. Death hath no more dominion over us.

HOLY SATURDAY – IN THE EVENING:
Waiting in hope

When I read of the great vigils that were such a feature of the worship of the early Church – whole nights spent in prayer, nights punctuated by chanted psalms, lengthy readings and fervent prayer – I wonder how it is that we can have reduced the drama of human redemption into something that can be set out in little more than an hour, certainly in less than two. A vigil is a watch. An alert waiting. The practice of expectant presence. The very word is related to watchfulness and to vigour. To keep vigil is the opposite of sleeping. Although it has come to be used in many and varied contexts, its original and primary use is ecclesiastical. Watchfulness was – and I hope still is – a mark of the Church.

I have, in time past, kept vigil through the night. Not in church but in hospital, watching, sometimes with others, sometimes alone, at a sickbed. I say 'sickbed' but it was a sickness unto death – and so we watched and waited – not as we do tonight for resurrection and new life, but for death, grim reaper or gentle Sister. As you sit and watch, alert to any change in the patient's condition, you are, I find, distracted at first, observing the coming and going of doctors and nurses, watching the monitors, counting the drips. As the hospital falls quiet, one might read a little, and pray – and the prayer is often, 'Lord, let it be quick' – but, more than anything else, watching a person, a living breathing human being, one thinks, meditates upon the weakness of flesh, upon our mortal condition, and upon the inevitability of death.

Perhaps this waiting for death is not quite so different from our own waiting for life. Holy Week requires a willing suspension of disbelief together with an exercise of imagination. Liturgy aids us in this. We were not just recalling Jesus' last supper with his disciples, we were there with him. We were in the Garden, in the courtyard outside Caiaphas's house, in the presence of the Roman governor. We were on Calvary's hill and witnessed the Passion and death of the beloved Lord Jesus, and we wept with his mother and his friends and disciples. Oh, we knew all along that he rose from death, but that death and the manner of his dying addresses powerfully and directly our mortality. And as we wait in liturgical vigil on this holy night, we are again confronted by the inevitability of death (and are thus reminded of where Lent began).

Two lines from hymns provide a graphic description. First, 'We three kings' – that jolly Christmas song has that one sombre verse which sings of the bitter perfume of myrrh:

> breathes a life of gathering gloom;
> sorrowing, sighing, bleeding, dying,
> sealed in the stone-cold tomb.

And then Sir Robert Grant's 'Saviour, when in dust to thee' – a solemn litany set to Joseph Parry's haunting and melancholy tune, Aberystwyth. It has disappeared from recent editions of hymn books but perhaps you recall its dramatic invocation of Christ's suffering:

> By thine hour of dire despair;
> By thine agony of prayer,
> By the Cross, the nail, the thorn,
> Piercing spear, and torturing scorn:
> By the gloom that veiled the skies
> O'er the dreadful Sacrifice.

Many of us have known despair. We have known the agony of prayer that echoes as it seems unheard. Though a physical spear may not have penetrated our flesh, we have known other things that have gone to the heart – depression, illness, disappointment, grief. Yes, here is Jesus in our humanity. Here is Jesus doomed to die. The Crucified. Even Jesus dies.

But Grant's last stanza has something more to say. At first it carries on from the skies veiled in gloom:

> By thy deep expiring groan;
> By the sad sepulchral stone.

Yes, here we are standing before the tomb. The stone put against it. The broken body of Jesus lying there in its shroud, stained already by blood from his head, his hands, his side, his feet. Here are the weeping women. Here are the terrified disciples. And Pilate broods in his palace and Caiaphas still does not rest easy in his house. But Grant takes us one step further:

> By the vault whose dark abode
> Held in vain the rising God.

This is it, this is what we have been waiting for. Grant has piled up the images of suffering and death, drawing them one after another from the Gospels, overwhelming us with tears, with pain, with grief – and all to no avail, for the borrowed tomb, the stone-cut vault guarded by soldiers and sealed by another great stone cannot hold the rising God. And our vigil does not end in death, but going through death we come to life.

This is the meaning of all we hear in tonight's vigil readings, the story of creation and fall, of sin and redemption. Noah is rescued by the saving ark floating on the waters of the flood. Israel, caught between Pharaoh's army and the waters of the Red Sea, crosses over from death to life. God initiates a new covenant and even dried-out bones can know new life.

We know that Christ is risen, but each Easter it bursts on us anew – like spring after winter. We cannot go straight to it, bypassing Good Friday. We need to grasp death, without fear, before we can grasp and be grasped by life, but one day our life's vigil will come to its own conclusion and we shall behold him whom the vault of death could not hold: the mighty risen and re-ascended Lord.

THE EASTER LITURGY:
Emerging from the labyrinth

On the afternoon of Easter Day, the dean of the cathedral of St Stephen at Auxerre received a ball from the newest of the canons. It was of such a size that it could be held in both hands. The dean tucked the ball under one arm and took the hand of the nearest priest. And he took the hand of the next priest and so on until a long chain was formed, possibly a circle. The dean intoned the *Victimae paschali laudes* and all joined in, accompanied by the organ – dean, canons, chaplains, vicars and clerks. The long chain of men performed a three-step dance round the great labyrinth laid in the floor of the nave at the extreme west end of the cathedral and the dean threw the ball alternately to the dancers. When all the singing and dancing was over, they hastened to a feast – wild boar, venison and hares were washed down with moderate quantities of red wine. And then all proceeded to evensong!

We are not entirely clear whether the dean or the canons traced the path of the labyrinth, the significance of which I discussed yesterday. But clearly the labyrinth, representing the complexity of life journeying toward death or the map of inextricable hell, was central, literally central to this dance. But what of the ball? Theseus, you recall, took with him a ball of pitch, with which he stopped the Minotaur's mouth, and a ball of thread which enabled him to find his way in and out of the labyrinth. In Christ's entry into the maze of hell, one commentator tells us, the ball of pitch was his humanity which caused the Devil to think that he was guilty of original sin and so subject to death and hell. As God cannot admit sin into the Divine Being, so Satan cannot take the sinless into hell and in trying to do so he violated the conditions of the infernal realm and lost his power over the justified. Christ's humanity was the ball that gagged Satan. The ball of thread was Christ's divinity, which permitted a safe retracing of the labyrinth and the rescue of the just souls within – the harrowing of hell and the resurrection. The ball-tossings in the Easter dance can then be seen as firmly grounded in the medieval Christian tradition and each participant helps towards the triumph over death by throwing the helpful ball.

And the third stanza of the sequence *Victimae paschali laudes* provides a fitting commentary:'*Mors et vita duello conflixere mirando: dux vitae mortuus, regnat vivus.*'

> Death with life contended: combat strangely ended!
> Life's own Champion, slain, yet lives to reign.

Labyrinth, sequence and dance together constitute a celebration performed by those saved by Christ from the labyrinth of hell, from the terror of death, through the mysteries of Easter. And our ordered liturgy, like that dance, imitates and invokes cosmic order and eternal bliss established by Christ in his death and resurrection.

EASTER DAY:
The Day of Resurrection

Alleluia! Christ is risen! This is the cry that fills the Church today, that shapes her life and gives voice to her joy for fifty days. Alleluia! Christ is risen! He is risen indeed! Alleluia! It is the source of our joy and of our hope that the Crucified Redeemer lives. Today is a day of joy. A day of good news, festive chant, sprinkled water of purification, solemn yet joyful liturgy, and the bonus of Easter eggs. It is a day in which hope has overcome reasoned and reasonable doubt, in which joy has displaced grief and in which light shows itself unconquered. As such it touches that part of us that believes, often against the odds, often in opposition to experience, that all will be well, in the long run, no matter how long the run may be.

It reveals that hope – a sure and certain hope, not something vague and ill-defined – is central to Christian faith. Christianity is not first and foremost about morality, about obeying rules or keeping commandments. It is not about being religious, talking in a special way, quoting biblical texts, differentiating the believing friend from the unbelieving, or asking, 'Are you saved?' It is not about the suspension of reason, the denial of intellect or the suppression of our critical faculties. It is also not about material or physical well-being.

It is about what it means to be human. It is about the way in which the Creator loves the creation and how creation and creatures acknowledge the Creator. It is about the mysteries of life; human creativity, suffering as both destructive and redemptive, how we become what we are intended to be, and what death means. It is about how God loves the world and suffers because we suffer, and how God came to share our human life and death. It is about a man who died a terrible death and who, against the odds, against all the evidence to the contrary, was found to be alive three days later. It is about the change in that man such that his broken body had become a glorious body though it still bore the marks of nails and spear.

Christianity requires of us first, faith, and a reasonable faith at that, belief and trust in God. Second, hope, that the darkest night will still end in dawn. Finally, love – love for God and love for one another, love such as that with which Christ loved us. It teaches us that the way that leads us to the fullness of our humanity is not easy. Why should it be? Is anything really worth doing easy? Why should Christian faith be easy? It teaches us that there may be, perhaps must be, suffering. We are reminded that the journey to this Easter Day comes by way of Good Friday. There is no resurrection without death. We may know our own deaths, and many of them, before we reach our last dying. We may know many resurrections before we come to the last one.

There is a spiritual experience of dying and rising; a dying to self and a rising to God, a dying to those aspects of this world that deny God and a rising to the values that affirm God. This process of death and resurrection is essential for our spiritual growth. But do not be mistaken. I am no unbelieving liberal, any more than I am a biblical fundamentalist. I affirm without reservation that Jesus of Nazareth was crucified, dead and buried, was sealed in the tomb, and rose again from the dead, passing through the vault of death. We are not to sub-stitute some spiritual or virtual reality for this. Dying and rising are real physical events. They are also an outward and visible expression of inward, invisible spiritual experiences.

It is possible to affirm the dying and rising of Jesus of

Nazareth and yet still say, so what? What we teach and affirm is that from the cross and the empty tomb comes a ray of light that penetrates into the darkest moments of our lives, a hope that is firm in the face of despair, a love from which we can never be separated. We can forget this. We often do. Today reminds us. It is not a day of complex theology and religious argument. It is a day of joy. A day of good news, festive chant, sprinkled water of purification, solemn yet joyful liturgy, Easter eggs and sure and certain hope of the glory that is yet to be revealed.

And so we reach the end. The evangelist Matthew gives us a splendidly dramatic account of the removal of the stone from before the sepulchre. The great stone, you will recall, was placed there by Joseph of Arimathea. Mary of Magdala and Mary the mother of James and Joseph were there. They witnessed the closing of the tomb as they sat opposite the sepulchre. Next came the officers of the chief priests. They sealed the tomb, fixing the stone in place, and they set a guard. That was the way it was last night. But toward dawn today, the first day of the week – for no matter what our diaries and calendars say, Sunday is still the first day of the week – the two Marys came to see the tomb. Matthew's dramatic moment, with its earthquake, the angelic descent and the rolling back of the stone, is not the moment of resurrection. It is the moment of revelation, of the opening of the tomb to reveal that the body of Jesus is no longer there. It has gone. The tomb is, in truth, empty.

The Gospel does not tell us *how* Christ was raised from the dead, only that he was. The Fathers of the Church delighted in finding a connection between the various outward signs of the resurrection. John Chrysostom, Bishop of Constantinople at the beginning of the fifth century, noticed parallels between Christ's birth and his resurrection. Christ was born from his mother's inviolate womb, so too he rose again from the closed tomb. He was the firstborn of his mother by birth, and the firstborn from the dead by resurrection. His birth did not break the seal of his mother's virginal integrity, and in his rising from the dead he did not break the seal set upon the tomb. And so, John continues, just as I cannot fully express his birth in words, neither can I wholly encompass his going forth from the tomb.

The resurrection is not an end in itself, rather it is the source of what follows. It unfolds the mystery of redemption. It cannot be understood in itself, but from it springs the new life of the baptised, nourished by eucharistic food. The outward signs are clear – water and washing, broken bread and eating, the sharing of a cup of wine. The inner reality, the dimension of grace, is hidden beneath but signified by the outward sign.

As you read this I hope that you have followed the liturgical, sacramental path through Holy Week, from the Palm Procession to the Easter Vigil and the joy of Easter Day. You will not then need me to remind you that the drama of the sign is important. The ritual splendour of the liturgical action is, literally, *significant*. The gospel signs – the earthquake and the radiant angelic presence – point to the reality of the resurrection, to the presence, soon to be encountered by the women, of the risen Christ himself. The innermost mystery of the resurrection is not available for our contemplation, only its fruits. We can speculate as much as we like about the *way* in which baptism incorporates us into Christ in his death and enables us to share in his resurrection. What is important is that it does, and it does so not because we know how but because we obey our Lord's command and fulfil the instructions that the apostles received from the Lord and handed on. Handing on is essential. 'Come and see,' says the angel, pointing to the empty tomb – the tomb, just opened, that could not hold the rising God. 'Go and tell,' said Jesus and that is precisely what our experience of Lent and Easter should enable us to do – to tell, to give an account of the hope that is in us, to witness to the saving death and glorious resurrection of our Lord and Saviour Jesus Christ.

DISCUSSION QUESTIONS

These questions could be used for discussion during the weeks of Lent. I have assumed that the reader will be at the liturgy throughout Holy Week and Easter.

Prologue to the First Saturday of Lent

1   In what ways can we ensure that Lent makes a difference to our daily living?
2   If you had just a few minutes to make a definitive testimony, what would you say?
3   What are the essentials that the Christian disciple needs to learn at the outset?

The First Week of Lent

4   Does it matter that there is an apparent connection between the stories in Genesis and Mesopotamian myths?
5   Should Noah have argued God out of flooding the world?
6   In what ways is our discipleship likely to be tested?
7   How can we give expression in our lives to being 'not my own but Christ's'?
8   What would be an appropriate Christian response to suffering and death?
9   Is it possible to hold both that God has 'stepped back from the creation' and that he answers prayers?

The Second Week of Lent

10 In the Bible the sovereign will of God often overrides ordinary morality; does it make it difficult for us to make moral judgements?

11 What can we learn from Abraham's experience of spiritual transformation?

12 Is it possible to believe in miracles today?

13 Is blind faith to be preferred to questioning faith?

14 'Israel's bondage is the type and symbol of human bondage.' To what extent do we experience sin as enslavement? How do we achieve liberation?

The Third Week of Lent

15 What methods can we use in seeking the sort of self-knowledge needed for confession?

16 Does the soul naturally aim at what it believes is good?

17 How can we promote what is good and true and beautiful without being labelled 'do-gooders' or religious fanatics?

18 What place does beauty have in our lives? How do we understand it?

19 Where is the boundary line between being prudent and living without real faith in the providence of God?

The Fourth Week of Lent

20 What is the purpose of our discipleship and our mission as disciples?

21 Have you done your duty when you have done what you think is your duty?

22 Should Christians reject status, honour, power, wealth and possessions?

23 Is there any aspect of Christian teaching that cannot be legitimately questioned?

24 Is there any value today in the traditional images of heaven and hell?

The Fifth Week of Lent

25 Is Jesus unfair to the chief priests, scribes and Pharisees?

26 Should we feel in anyway threatened by the parable of the vineyard?

27 Are there any real risks involved in being a disciple of Jesus today?

28 Science tells us a great deal about the possible origin of life on earth. Scripture constantly reaffirms that we are 'dust returning to dust'. Can we hold both the scientific and scriptural views?

29 If the path of discipleship seems easy, have we gone the wrong way?

QUOTATION SOURCES

p. xii Book of Common Prayer, Church Hymnal Corporation, New York, 1979.

p. 22 Leo the Great, Sermon 27, On the Festival of the Nativity 7.

p. 85 Eric Zencey, *Panama*, Hodder, 1996.

p. 90 The additional verse to Christopher Wordsworth's hymn 'Songs of thankfulness and praise' is by F. Bland Tucker, from *The Hymnal 1982*, © Church Pension Fund, New York, used by permission.

The quotation from Dante is from *The Divine Comedy: Paradise*, canto XXIII, lines 31–3, translated by Dorothy L. Sayers and Barbara Reynolds, © Penguin Books, 1962, used by permission.

p. 103 The source of this quotation from St Ambrose, jotted down in one of my notebooks, escapes me.

p. 113 John of Ford, *Sermons on the final verses of the Song of Songs*, Cistercian Publications, Kalamazoo, 1982.

pp. 130–3 This meditation uses information from Penelope Reed Doob, *The Idea of the Labyrinth from Classical Antiquity through the Middle Ages*, Cornell University Press, Ithaca, New York, 1990.